INTEGRATED MANAGEMENT SYSTEM
Combining other standards with ISO 9001

By Frede Jensen

Integrated Management System:
Combining other standards with ISO 9001

First edition

Copyright © 2017 Frede Jensen

All rights reserved

Cover by the author

Published by the author; distributed through lulu.com

Lulu.com book ID: 19537512

ISBN: 978-1-326-81090-0

Contents

Introduction 1
   What is a management system? 3
   What should be integrated? 4
   Functional vs process team groupings? 5
   Why should we adopt standards? 10
Management system model 13
   Organisational context 16
   Where do policy, objectives and KPIs fit in? 18
   Process approach 19
Leadership 22
   Leader competence and confidence 23
Planning 24
   Plan development and deployment 24
      Setting targets 28
Operation and support 29
   Operation 29
   Support 30
      People 30
      Facilities 30
      Documentation in processes 31
Performance evaluation 32
   Measurement 32
   Auditing 33
      Self-checks 34
   Management review 35

- Improvement 36
  - Evidence-based decision making 38
  - Analysis 40
  - Proactive and reactive actions 41
- Suppliers 42
- Customers and interested parties 44
  - Customer needs 44
  - Customer satisfaction 45
  - What level of dissatisfaction will people tolerate? 48
- Standards 50
  - Management system standards 51
  - ISO 9001 52
  - ISO 14001 54
  - ISO 50001/EN 16001 55
  - OHSAS 18001 56
- Integrated processes documentation 57
- Process design 61
- Risk and opportunity 65
  - Risk management 66
  - Failure Mode and Effects Analysis 67
  - Business Continuity 70
    - Emergency Response Plan 71
- Managing people-based systems 72
  - Corporate values statement 73
  - Self-managing units 74
    - Team board 75
- Glossary and definitions 78
- Appendix 81

Preface

It is easy to get deep into the details of implementing a management system standard, such as ISO 9001, without achieving its overall intent. The main benefits from management standards come from foremost thinking in terms of the overall model. This is particularly important when implementing multiple standards together, because implementing the details of one system, in isolation, can potentially undo or mask the wider importance of details in another system. The bigger picture should be defined and combined first, before we start addressing the finer details of the mixed requirements.

The effective management of processes is only half the system. More precisely, it is the foundation half. Excellence comes from the inventiveness and customer relationship activities that we operate on top of this foundation. Nonetheless, the management system underpins everything and is therefore an essential prerequisite for excellence to occur.

Beware, it is possible to over-manage people. A bad system will put people in straightjackets and switch off their inherent motivation for providing excellence. A good system will provide people with the means to prevent doing wrong, and simultaneously provide a supporting platform from which they can use their discretionary talent for doing right. In a way, the management system must simultaneously prevent the occurrence of unmanageable variation and allow the occurrence of manageable variation. Confused?

Frede Jensen, London 2017

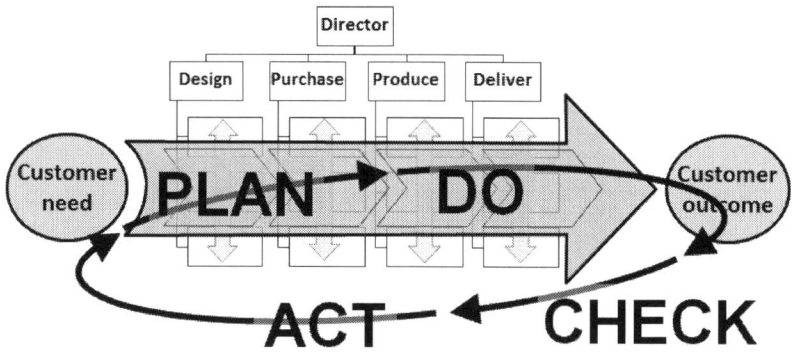

More resources at

www.deopmanagement.com

Introduction

The ability to 'think in action' and to plan eventualities on an ad-hoc basis, as and when we encounter them, is an admirable human quality. However, it is a poor primary approach to management. Lacking resolve on the underlying root causes of variability in work processes will mean that the system is not advancing. It is forever re-living the same repeat difficulty issues. There is little joy in being a customer to a haphazard 'thinking in action' management approach, with its higher probability for oversights and for encountering problems. Lack of proactive systematic management, on average, yields less success and low efficiency.

There exists a multitude of recognised standards and regulations for the many different sorts of management systems focussing on different subject areas and components of an organisation. The objectives in one subject area will mostly complement other objectives of the organisation, such as those relating to quality, financial results, the environment and occupational health and safety. The different management standards therefore tend to all have a degree of overlap and repetition between them. Implementing them in isolation of each other, in a bolted together approach, results in duplication inefficiencies and potentially creates needlessly conflicting approaches. When you want to optimally address all standards at once and overall best plan the organisation's resources allocation then you plain and simply need to establish a single Integrated Management System, aligning all the different subject areas and components to the common organisational purpose.

The term 'integrated' in this context means combined into a coherently interrelated whole, as opposed to co-existing as parallel entities. An **Integrated Management System combines all the components of an organisation into one coherent response to the full purpose and mission of the organisation.**

Integrated management is a concept wherein functional responsibilities are dispersed, but not segregated, throughout the organisation. For example, the production manager has a share in the quality, environmental, safety and financial responsibilities. The various process components for addressing quality, environmental, safety and financial management in his/her functional area of responsibility are defined in a single common device. The organisation may have a quality lead or co-ordinator or a governance function, for example, but such role is not treated as a separate specific function. The responsibilities for managing quality should be integrated across all functions within the organisation, in effect acting as one coherent function.

Anything that is managed separately and independently of other organisational components is not integrated. Simply placing the quality manager, environmental manager and safety manager in the same department is not integration. Simply placing all quality, environmental and safety documentation alongside each other in one all-encompassing manual is not integration. They are not integrated until they form one coherent management system.

The International Standards Organisation (ISO) has made a Directive, Annex SL, prescribing a universal High Level Structure (HLS) and core language to be shared across all its future management systems standards. The HLS has been implemented in its ISO 9001:2015, for example. It will take some years before HLS is implemented in all the existing management system standards; but this does not prevent their immediate integration with any HLS based standard. The system model presented in this book is compatible with both the HLS and historic standards.

WHAT IS A MANAGEMENT SYSTEM?

There are several sources and variants of definitions. Firstly, we could look at the ISO definitions: "[Ed.] *A set of interrelated or interacting elements of the organisation that formulate policies and objectives. The management system elements further establish the organisation's structure, roles and responsibilities, planning, operation, practices, rules, priorities, beliefs, information flows, processes and changes that are needed to achieve those policies and objectives. The scope or focus of a management system could be limited to a specific function or subject area of the organisation or it could include the entire organisation*".

Secondly, we could look at what are in the words. The picture here below defines 'Manage' as to "*develop, deploy and monitor resources with a purpose*". Each of the terms making up this definition further have their own definitions, as shown. The management system has an inferred feedback loop, in the "*monitor*" element referring back to the "*develop*" element, for advancing the system towards its intended "*aim*".

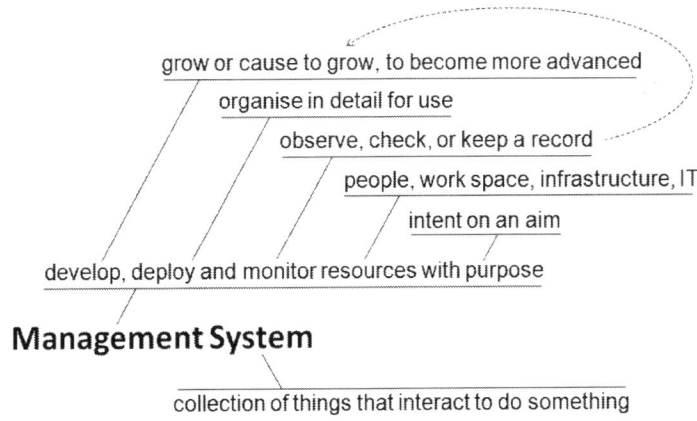

The management systems definitions and requirements for various specific subject areas of an organisation can be found in recognised National or International Standards. The following table lists some example subject area labels and standards. Every organisation is likely to focus on its own specifically relevant set. The model presented in this book does not integrate the adopted standards themselves into one, but instead it kind of groups them into a collection. The notion of an all-encompassing integrated standard is too big and complex to contemplate. Instead, it is the implementation response to the chosen collection of separate standards that effectively 'integrates' them into one system.

Subject area	Typical management system label
Quality	Quality Management System, such as defined by standard ISO 9001.
Environment	Environmental Management System, such as defined by standard ISO 14001.
Energy	Energy Management System, such as defined by standard ISO 50001/EN 16001.
Occupational Health & Safety	Occupational Health and Safety Management System, such as defined by OHSAS 18001.
Food safety	Food Safety Management System (e.g. for a food producer), such as defined by ISO 22000.
Business Continuity	Business Continuity Management System, such as defined by standard ISO 22301.
Data security	Information Security Management System, such as defined by standard ISO 27001.
Assets	Assets Management System, such as defined by requirements standard ISO 55001.
Finance	Finance Management System, such as defined in various financial Regulations and codes.
Simultaneous Quality, Environment, OH&S, Finance and others	**Integrated Management System**, such as defined by the combination of different standards and regulatory requirements.

WHAT SHOULD BE INTEGRATED?

Any area or component of an organisation that influences the outcome or result for the organisation should belong in the Integrated Management System. This means all formal activities for managing quality, environment, energy, data security, safety, finance etc. Processes and their documentation should combine all the systems components into one coherent system. Integration comes about by introducing a combined practice, in place of multiple separate practices. For example, the quality audit process, environmental audit process and safety audit process are combined into a single audit process that simultaneously verifies quality, environmental and safety performance.

All areas and components of an organisation should as a minimum share the following common system processes in a single combined operating manual:

- Organisational planning: objectives, risk and resilience.
- Customer and regulatory requirements management.
- Responsibilities, accountability and authority.
- Management review.
- Operational processes.
- Performance evaluation and improvement.
- Competence, training, awareness and participation.
- Programme management.
- Suppliers relationships management
- Documents and records control.
- Internal auditing.
- Proactive and reactive correction processes.

FUNCTIONAL VS PROCESS TEAM GROUPINGS?

Fact of the matter is that customers do not care much for what goes on inside an organisation. They raise a need and simply expect to receive a corresponding outcome in return. But this customer perspective is seldom what is foremost being discussed day-to-day inside the organisation. Although all the different operational areas have an overall common goal, they can often have differing and possibly even conflicting day-to-day aims. People with experience in organisations may recognise discussions similar to the following. Design manager: *"I need this new part from a new supplier"*. Purchasing manager: *"No, I won't buy it because it conflicts with my goal of reducing the supplier-base and obtaining overall best pricing for everything else"*. Production manager: *"I can't worry about what part you select, because my immediate focus is on improving our production schedule"*. Delivery manager: *"I don't really care for what you all do, as long you design something that helps me cost-optimise the loading of my delivery vehicles"*. All statements are valid and important, but they are not coherent or collaborative. They are disjointed.

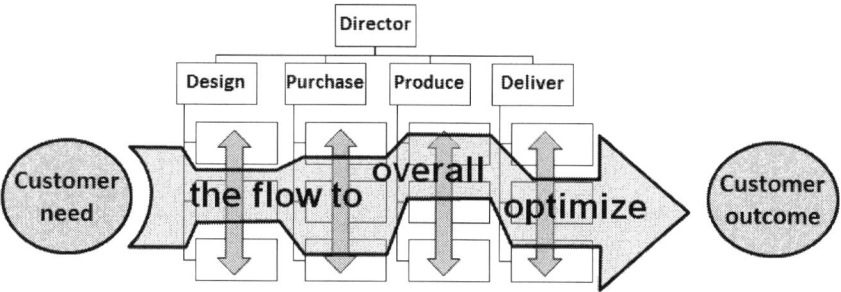

Process optimisation result within a non-integrated organisation.

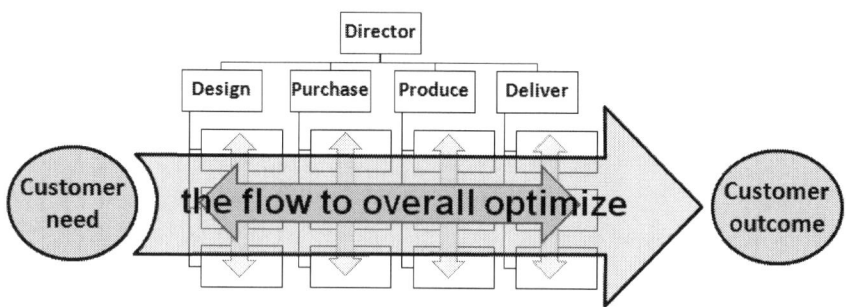

Process optimisation result within an integrated organisation.

We can define an organisation as integrated or non-integrated, in terms of how its teams collaborate on transforming customer input requirements into a corresponding output – i.e. transforming needs into outcomes. In the non-integrated organisation, the activities are divided per the organisational structure. This results in narrower procedural thinking, handovers, duplication of efforts and in tasks being optimised in isolation of the wider purpose. This is referred to as a silo mentality. From the customers' perspective, they will perceive an organisation that has an internal focus and thereby becomes static to the evolving requirements – because customer needs reside outside the organisation and they are forever changing.

Instead of thinking of the organisation as a structure of departments, we should learn to also think of it as the core process that flows across it. This enables us to better focus on the customer, at the start and end of the organisation's overall purpose, and to be responsive to the forever changing needs. The organisation can be looked at as a value-chain that end-to-end interlinks the customer input (need) with the product output (outcome). Improvement is about continually and collaboratively enhancing what adds value, while reducing or eliminating what does not. This is particularly true when implementing multiple systems standards that overlap.

Organisational units within the core flow must share and align to a common goal, to enable focus on the customer at the start and end of the process, and to be responsive to the forever changing needs. The concept falls apart when any one unit emphasises its own goals above those of the whole – i.e. seeking to maximise its own performance in isolation of the wider objectives, even when this is perhaps done with well-meaning intentions towards the customer. The actions within any one sub-unit should not become a burden up- or down-stream to itself. This may mean, at times, making one's own activity less efficient, or taking on or giving away responsibilities, where this benefits the greater purpose of improving the overall system outcomes.

Process workers may be grouped by their functions – e.g. the design team is grouped and led by an expert designer. However, the concept of team is wider than simply the functional grouping. Team is also the chain of functions across the organisation, transforming the customer input requirements into a corresponding product. The designer is just as much team with purchasing, production and delivery colleagues, as he or she is with other designers. Any weakness or support need within the total chain is everyone's problem.

> **Grouping the teams by their functional structure is good for optimising the pooled competencies and skills scheduling and efficiency.**

> **Grouping, or integrating, the teams per the core flow across the organisation is the good for optimising customer-focus and processes interlinking.**

The integrated flow-centred team grouping can feel more abstract, compared to the physical organisational team-structures, and is therefore more easily overlooked. However, it is what makes the organisation responsive to customers and organisational requirements. Care must be taken that the structural/functional team does not over-rule or de-emphasize the integrated flow-centred team.

In practice, we need to apply both team concepts. Every person within the organisation belongs to both a functional structure and to a process structure. For example, if we teamed up per the process flow alone, and ignored the functional structure, then we may lose the critical mass for like-minded competencies getting together and creating the next new thing. By nature of customer aspirations, pure customer responsiveness will mostly lead to incremental improvement only. Innovation comes from people temporarily looking outside the day-to-day demands and start thinking up new ways of fulfilling yet unrealised customer needs that are not yet being demanded. If we did solely what the customer asks for then there may be an optimised flow, but there would be little structural re-design and innovation. The optimised flow may meet current customer requirements, but it would never in the longer term exceed expectations or excite customers. Some specification can only be found or created outside the core process flow. There are periods, ranging from minutes to days, where we must step out of the process flow, to take time to think beyond the immediate customer expectations.

An example relates to society's rising health expectations, coinciding with economic austerity and healthcare skills shortages. This has over the last decade given rise to a trend in which health services across the world have felt forced to divide up specialist departments per the workflows. In some hospitals, the treatment of patients with respiratory difficulties, for example, has been divided into three workflows, according to severity. Mild cases are no longer admitted to the specialist department, but are instead treated in a general care unit. The most severe cases of respiratory distress are transferred away to a fewer number of highly skilled regional centres of excellence. The remaining original specialist department continues to receive about the middle third of patients. The fragmentation of the specialist area into three smaller thirds makes it more difficult to efficiently schedule the individual workflows, such as flexibly covering night shifts, holidays and unplanned staff absenteeism. It is further suggested that it has become more difficult to develop and maintain skills, because of the loss of insight and cross-fertilised thinking within the wider peer group. The best skilled staff, exposed to nothing but the most distressing cases, become prone to higher sickness rates and burning out. Hence, the improvement from establishing a customer-centric workflow has in this case become negated by reduced resources effectiveness.

WHY SHOULD WE ADOPT STANDARDS?

Any organisation that has activities intended on assuring a planned outcome, or simply to limit any adversely different outcome, can be said to have a management system. The management system, whether formal or informal, is fundamental to succeeding and practically all organisations have one. The degree of formality and effort going into the management system is often a commercial decision, weighing the perceived costs and benefits.

Standards are fundamentally designed for voluntary use. Some standards, however, can become mandatory by regulatory 'harmonization' – e.g. a standard becomes referenced in a legal instrument, as a means for demonstrating legal conformity across a sector or geographical region. Harmonization simplifies compliance and verification processes – i.e. it reduces an industry sector's overall compliance costs.

Standards are strategic tools that help the organisation assure it is doing right, in meeting recognised acceptable levels of performance and safety, thereby minimising mistake costs and the potential consequences from non-conformity with legal requirements. This, it is argued, provide a basis for sustainability. Most organisations, however, tend to adopt a standard simply for marketing purposes and because its customers expect it.

Adopting a standard is not a one-off activity, but it has a life-cycle of continual improvement in outcomes. Initially, the adopting organisation creates a platform for conforming to the standard requirements, and from which it can improve.

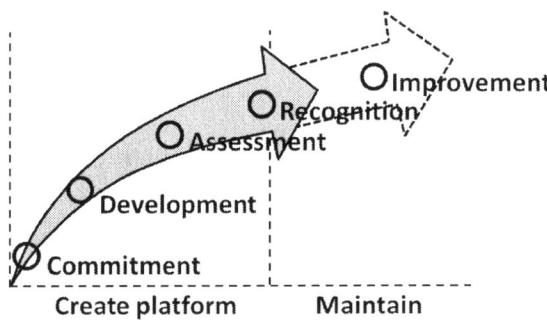

The language and generic nature of a standard's text can appear somewhat non-representational of its practical application. The translation of the, at times mind-numbing, texts into practical use tends to demand a degree of experience. It is something that we typically must get wrong a few times, before we have gained sufficient understanding to be able to apply with success. This book is intended to be more closely representative of the practical world and to pass on a good portion of that needed experience.

Even when we get through the initial learning experiences in adopting a standard that is new to us, there are some potentially persisting difficulties to be mindful of:

Warning 1: The prerequisite for adopting a voluntary standard is a willingly receptive organisation. The standard presents a sound model for a system, but it does not necessarily resolve all ills. The model has a reduced chance of success if the organisation, and its top management in particular, does not believe in it. Attempting to bolt an external standard on to an inherently dysfunctional organisation that is incapable of changing its poor practices can possibly make matters worse, by introducing an added burden of work and complexity in pursuit of something the organisation will not be able to meet or properly maintain anyway.

<u>Warning 2:</u> If a standard is likely to become compromised by an overreaching priority of a higher strategy objective or another more important standard then, whether or not the organisation believes in it, the subordinate standard may never become effectively integrated and it will instead risk becoming a half-hearted bolt-on to the organisation's present true focus. In such case, it may be best not to commit to the standard in full, but instead adopt its most important principles more loosely, less formally. For example, if an organisation is in financial distress then it may not be a good time to fully embark on the adoption of an environmental management standard. That is unless the formal certification to the standard is key to, say, accessing new business and thereby resolving the financial situation.

<u>Warning 3:</u> The risk management controls for a standard implementation must not become a straightjacket that prevents advancing the organisation. Conformity to a pre-defined standard is intended to assure against doing wrong. In practice, however, yesterday's standard will often lack behind today's evolving and personalised needs. Conformity to a standard is therefore not necessarily a guarantee that we are continually and always doing right. We generally learn more from our failures than we do from our successes. When things go wrong, first we fix it and then we learn the lesson to prevent a recurrence. Elimination of all risk-taking could potentially stifle learning and make the organisation static. Risk is therefore not necessarily all bad – as long it is properly evaluated and it remains manageable. The integrated management system must simultaneously facilitate the assurance of conformity to established external standards and facilitate the opportunity for ongoing creation of the organisation's own new standards. This demands that there is room for sensible deviation and learning within the management system, through allowance of a manageable amount of risk. It is therefore important that the system managers understand the meaning of risk-based decisions.

Management system model

The model is centred on the Plan-Do-Check-Act (PDCA) cycle, which originates from the 1950's Shewhart Cycle and was since popularised by Edward Deming. In a subsequent variant, Deming replaced the control-centric 'Check' element with the more progressive term 'Study'. In this book we retain the term 'Check', as it is currently expressed in the international standards, but we will in fact apply it more as a study activity – meaning to measure, investigate and analyse. The PDCA cycle provides the underlying plan for our management activities and the continual improvements of the management system.

Plan:
Establish objectives, processes and resources to deliver results and to address risk and opportunity.

Do:
Implement the plan; operate and support the process to realize the product and service.

Act:
Analyse to determine causes of deficiencies. Take actions to improve performance.

Check:
Monitor, study, chart and evaluate the performance and outcomes against the target objectives. Report the result.

Definitions for the PDCA cycle elements.

The PDCA cycle is obvious enough, but how do we build an integrated system around it? In essence, we integrate the multiple management standards by:

1. Creating a universal model that can be used to represent any standard and will incorporate all their requirements; and then

2. Implementing the detailed requirements from the multiple management systems standards within this single model.

The universal model presented in this book is based on the International Standards Organisation's ISO 9001. It enables the management of different standards, activities, resources, relationships and responsibilities all within one system. The model contains 5 internal elements and 1 external element, all evolving around the PDCA cycle, namely: Leadership, Planning, Operation and support, Suppliers (the external element), Performance evaluation and Improvement. The Operation process is typically a series of inter-linked or inter-connected sub-processes performed across various organisational functions, such as, for example, design, procurement, production and delivery.

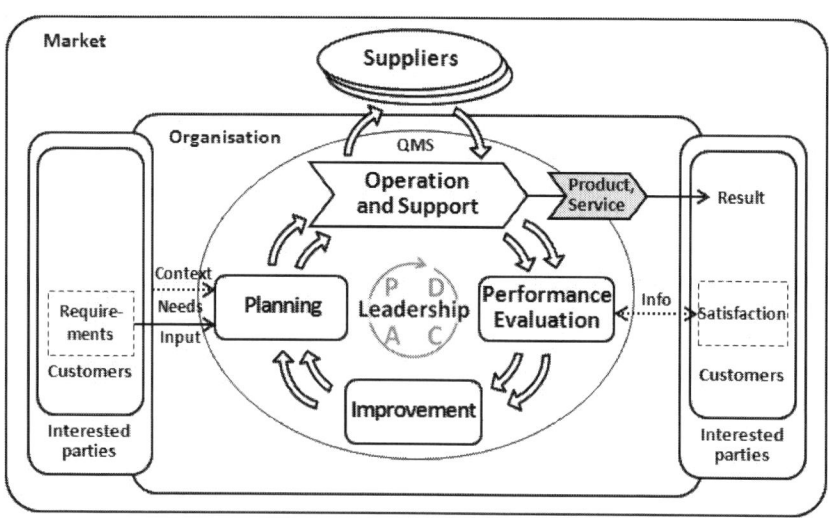

Integrated management system model

Leadership and the PDCA cycle in fact occur at multiple levels, represented here by a series of two parallel arrows; where the outer arrows represent senior management taking a strategic view and where the inner arrows represent self-managing teams taking a tactical/procedural view on the system. Senior managers plan and operate in outline terms, whereas the teams will plan and operate the related details. **The successful outcome for the organisation and its customers depends on the effectiveness of both the 'strategic' and the 'tactical' PDCA cycles.**

The purpose of the 5+1 system elements can be summarised as:

Leadership
Drives the effective implementation and ongoing execution of the PDCA cycle across the system. Sets a unified direction and promotes the coherence to planned objectives. Unblocks any obstacles and maintains conditions for achieving the objectives.

Planning
Determines the customer input, mandatory requirements and the organisational context, for translation into objectives. The context will influence the objectives for making use of opportunities for improvement and efficiencies as they arise. Planning also considers and incorporates countermeasures to any risks of deviation from the objectives.

Operation and support
Organise and control the multiple activities and linkages in the processes-chain and resources, for purpose of producing the planned result – e.g. transform the input requirements into a corresponding output. The support element develops and maintains the appropriate competencies, capability and capacity in people, equipment, infrastructure and work environment.

Performance Evaluation
Measures, investigates and analyses the processes, product and outcomes, including customer satisfaction, for purpose of

verifying that planned results are met and for identifying new risks and opportunities. Periodic audits objectively measure effectiveness and verify ongoing conformity to requirements.

<u>Improvement</u>
Reactive and proactive activity for assuring the ability to meet requirements and for enhancing the satisfaction of customers and other interested parties. Improvement relies on evidence-based decision making.

<u>Suppliers</u>
Suppliers are not part of the organisation, but they can influence outcomes and can thereby be considered as part of the wider system. In some industries, suppliers are equally or more important to the results than the organisation's own resources are. Suppliers should therefore be engaged with similar attentiveness as given to the organisation's own resources.

The term 'system' is defined as a **collection of things that interact to do something**. The 5+1 elements in our model are doing something together and interact with an end-to-end focus on the outcome meeting the requirements that originate from customers and other interested parties. In the day-to-day routine, the organisation may take a narrower processing view on simply transforming the input orders into a corresponding product. The basis for improvement is that we now-and-then take the fuller perspective on the system, and study the actual outcomes that our product and service produce – in terms of customer satisfaction or environmental impact, for example. The management review now-and-then also involves a deeper study and consideration of the detailed requirements and market context.

ORGANISATIONAL CONTEXT
The context is defined by the organisation's state of development, relative to the expectations upon it. The risk from not knowing

the context is the organisation's misperception of its shortfall in achieving the true needs and priorities, which can result in inadequate planning and failure. It is important to be realistic in the understanding of what the organisation self and its wider interested parties require from the management system. The organisation should continually monitor and keep up-to-date with its context.

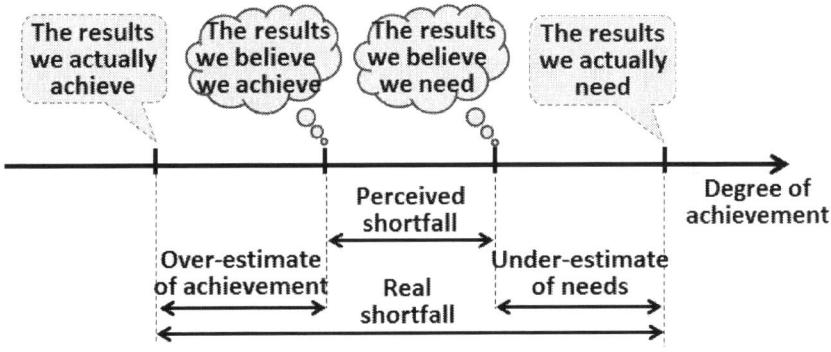

Misalignment between perception and reality

Understanding the context involves discovering and defining the issues that influence the organisation's objectives and its ability to achieve the planned results. Some of the questions the organisation may ask itself when seeking to discover issues in its context are:

- Do we really understand our market?
- Do we have sufficient insight on our customers, their needs, plans, problems and anxieties?
- Do we have sufficient insight on our interested parties, their needs, plans, problems and anxieties?
- Do we understand our own capabilities?
- Do we know what we want?

- Do we know who can give us what we want, and do we know what of equally perceived worth they want from us in return?
- What is the picture that we want us self to look like?
- Our key people, who make things happen, to what extent have they bought into the picture of what we want to look like?
- Do we know precisely where we are in respect of the picture, including the rate of progress – i.e. when can we get there?

These are not one-off questions, but they should periodically be re-assessed. There will be many sources of context issues, both internal and external. Some external interested parties can have major influences on the organisational context. For example, they may be shareholders in a private company specifying certain commercial performance expectations; or they may be a regulatory authority specifying a mandatory standard. Context issues will also arise from market dynamics, performance benchmarks, employee values, technology, and the social, cultural and economic operating environments – whether they local or global.

WHERE DO POLICY, OBJECTIVES AND KPIS FIT IN?

Policy and objectives provide the organisation with a planned direction and focus, to assist it in applying its resources with a constancy of purpose. By attaching targets, or Key Performance Indicators (KPIs), and responsibilities for their implementation, the policy and its objectives also become the over-reaching framework for performance management. The KPIs are needed as a reference measure in the 'performance evaluation' element of the PDCA-based system.

Policy is simply a statement of the overall aims and objectives which are appropriate for the organisation's purpose and context, and which the organisation has committed to. The policy statement is communicated to all relevant people in the organisation and relevant interested parties. There will be many sources of policy, both internal and external, such as the organisation's strategy, standards and regulations. In the integrated management system, the diverse policies should ideally be brought together into a single statement or document. This is to ensure their compatibility and collective effectiveness.

KPIs are cascaded down from strategy and policy objectives (see more on this in the "Plan development and deployment" section later). The fulfilment of the KPIs in effect drives the policy implementation. The various roles, responsibilities and authorities for implementing the objectives and KPIs must be clearly assigned and understood.

PROCESS APPROACH

A process is *"an activity or set of activities using resources, and are managed to enable the transformation of inputs into outputs"*. Generally, the output from one process forms the input to the next. The process should therefore be considered as part of an extended interlinking value-chain – starting and ending with the customer and other interested parties.

The term 'process approach' refers to the *"systematic definition and management of processes and their interactions so that to achieve the intended overall results in accordance with policies and strategy direction of the organisation"* [source: ISO 9001].

The process approach enables the organisation managing the system and its value creation as an integrated whole, including the risks and opportunities that span across the organisation. The PDCA cycle is central in managing the approach and its processes, by contributing to the organisation's effectiveness and efficiency in continually enhancing its overall performance.

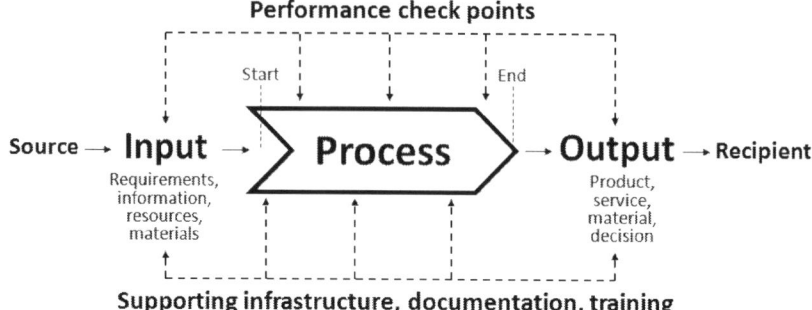

Single process model (adapted from ISO 9001:2015).

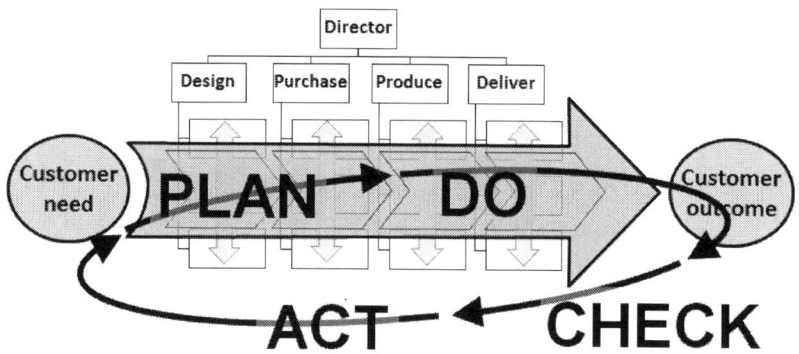

Process approach, integrating multiple processes.

A process is defined by describing the step-by-step tasks that it performs, together with their interactions with the various elements shows in the 'single process model' diagram above. The definition should also identify who is responsibility for performing and overseeing the process. The process definition may be expressed in a process chart, which has some result criteria attached – i.e. definition should be telling: "*This is how we want to perform the activity and this is what we want the output to look like*". In this way, everyone can be clear about the tasks and how they link to the organisation's objectives.

To use the process approach, the organisation should understand and define the processes that are important to its objectives. The definitions should appropriately balance both risks and opportunities within the system overall. For example, defining a 'performance check point' may help prevent a deviance from the original intent and, thereby, protect against a failure happening. However, if this control is over-rigidly defined then it may simultaneously prevent an opportunity for improving the process, by not allowing or by de-motivating a potentially useful deviation from a new value-enhancing idea. Sometimes it is better to build assurance against deviation in to the processes inter-linking – i.e. check the process inputs and/or outputs, but do not perform checks within the process itself. This avoids restricting any new opportunities from being taken within. The number of check points shown in our 'single process model' here are simply to illustrate what may be. It is preferable for a process be so well developed and implemented that its performance does not depend on any checks at all. Only use a check point if there is a real lack of confidence in the activity or where we must produce and record a measure, for use in the ongoing performance evaluation or for, say, legal evidence and traceability reasons.

The systemic process approach further has an asset management purpose. ISO 55000 on asset management defines an asset as *"something that has potential value to an organisation and for which the organisation has a responsibility"*. Knowledge and information held in systems and processes are assets. It is accessible, secure and relatively low in cost. By contrast, knowledge and information held in individual people can be a liability. We can lose it; the information flow is slowed and distorted by gate-keeper politics; and we must continually compensate and stimulate the individual to use it.

Leadership

The manager and the leader are often the same person, who adapts his or her behaviour to differing situations. Defining a system is often the easiest part of managing. The difficulty lays in the system's effective implementation and ongoing operation. Leadership is about inspiring energy, commitment and cohesion amongst the people influencing the product of the system. This is in part achieved by establishing a connection between customer needs and people's own personal needs, and by promoting good practices. When difficulties or exceptions arise, the leader role is needed to step in to unblock the obstacles and direct people through the situation.

Manager	Leader
• Seeks longer term result	• Seeks shorter term result
• Depends on systems	• Depends on people
• Is assigned subordinates	• Establishes followers
• Issues instructions	• Inspires people to act

Leaders as managers are engaged in activities at all levels within the organisation – i.e. they are engaged in all activities within the management system. On busy days, you will find the nominated manager showing leadership by helping in stacking shelves and taking customer telephone calls. Other times the manager is developing resources, such as selecting new machinery, recruiting and training people. Managers have yet another function, as members of the organisations top leader team, performing the management system reviews for purpose of consistently meeting all the various needs and ensuring that risks and opportunities are addressed.

Day-to-day leader actions involve 'digging out' the individual employees' values and then show their important contribution to the overall success – and to add a "thank you". Customers need something similar. Frontline employees should use leadership techniques or key words to trigger the customers' awareness of their own personal values and then emphasise the organisation and its system's compatibility with those customer values.

LEADER COMPETENCE AND CONFIDENCE

People are naturally drawn to and follow (well placed) self-confidence. It is perceived as a position of strength, which people want to join-in with and feel part of. Self-confidence comes from being allowed to succeed. Self-confidence gives leaders the strength to be assertive when needed, because people naturally accept and subscribe to the strength. Self-confidence and ability to be assertive (when needed) are thereby the signs of a succeeding competent leader. The flip side is when these important attributes are conveyed by an incompetent leader, when they translate into their bywords arrogance and bullying. The latter two attributes are a sure sign of incompetence, which people and customers will not follow.

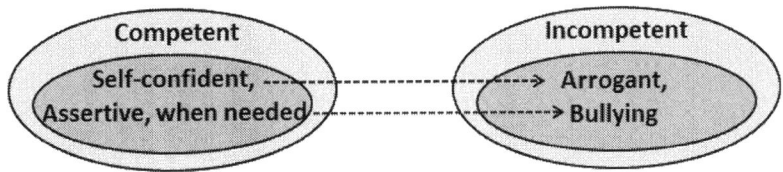

Planning

Planning is about identifying and establishing actions that will appropriately and adequately address the requirements and the associated risks and opportunities. The plan defines measurable objectives, including what, when and who (what resources) will do something.

Plan Development and Deployment

The development and deployment of the strategic plan is a process, which cascades down a set of organisational objectives and policies for implementation. Even with the best possible context information, inputs into the planning process are typically incomplete and invariably based on a degree of assumptions about the causal links between initiatives and their effects. The forecasted effects from initiatives can therefore not be entirely validated in advance of implementing the plan and they will invariably need continual monitoring and correcting.

The strategic plan development and deployment process starts by asking the fundamental questions of: *"What is it that we want"? "Who can realistically give it to us"?* And, *"how can we get them to give it to us; what would they want from us in exchange"?* The term *"Who"* here includes markets, customers, employees, managers, facilities and systems. Once we have determined the answers, then the process is to define a set of objectives for making the exchange happen. The strategic objectives are subsequently cascaded down for implementation at a tactical level. Deploying the objectives involves identifying their 'critical success factors' (CSF), to which are attached measures and targets – sometimes termed 'key performance indicators' (KPI). A CSF is defined as an element in the final situation, which would demonstrate that an objective is successfully met. The CSFs and their KPIs in effect 'operationalise' the organisation's strategy. The strategic level receives monitoring reports from both the tactical and procedural levels, to enable its continual validation, or re-thinking, of the original strategy assumptions. The pendulum analogy highlights the importance of good strategic planning, by illustrating how a unit of effort at the strategy level has a greater impact on output than a unit of effort at the tactical/procedural level. It is not something an organisation would want to get wrong.

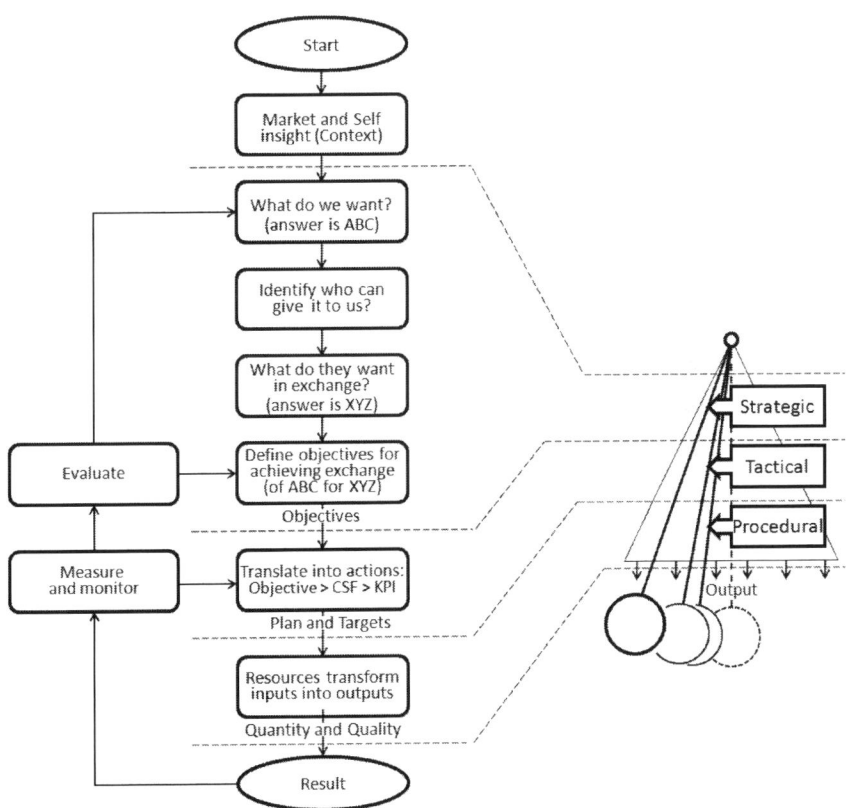

Plan development and deployment process

Aims		Objectives	Critical Success Factor	Key Performance Indicator
Operating Year 2016: • Grow turnover 15% • Net margin 5% • Financial sustainability over the longer term • Deliver value for money and quality, from a mid-position, price-benefit approach (appealing to mass-market) Last review date: 01/01/2016	Finance	• Expand customer-base 15%	New corporate partners joining	8 corporate partners by Jan 2017
		• Improve prices by 1%	Expand products variety, at manageable neutral cost	120 catalogue lines Jan 2017
		• Improve relative cost efficiency by 5%	Enter new market	1 new export market with >5m population by Jan 2017
		• Reduce exposure to risk from changes in sales mix	Increase in productivity	Lean review by July 2016 identifying >£100k waste reduction
			Consolidate strategic suppliers base	10 strategic suppliers by Jan 2017
			Determine cost break-down for all activities, and consistently align with service charges	Re-calculate ABC for all activates by May 2016, available for pricing reviews. Improve average sell price 1%
	Customer	• Know customer needs	Measure and monitor real customer needs/satisfaction	Annual customer satisfaction survey. Score >98% good rating
		• Understand key market drivers (who they are and their influences)	Knowing and understanding market drivers	Attend at least 2 industry/trade event per year
			Establish knowledgebase of competing products	By June 2016. Maintain, evolve and use throughout year
		• Launch 1 new product for every 20 in catalogue	Exposure article in national publication	Publish articles combined reaching >75% partners in 2016
		• Add 1 service enhancement	On-line shop	Accept sales and despatch from beginning Aug 2016
		• Be leader in customer satisfaction	Establish 6 new products, pre-Christmas	6 new products on sale by end-Oct 2016
			Establish refurbishment exchange service	Generic exchange product in catalogue from Jul 2016
	Process	• Fulfil orders on time and accurately	Meet promises on order turnaround time	>98% on-time next day class deliveries, measured monthly
				>95% on-time 3-day deliveries, measured monthly
				>90% exchanged made within 2 days, measured monthly
				<3 stock out events per month, measured monthly
		• Robust handling of variability, exceptions and complexity	High quality yield	Quality yield >96%, measured monthly
		• Exceed industry operating standards in areas where it supports a claim to be best-in-class	Maintain standard requirements	Maintain ISO 9001 certification in 2016
		• Maintain quality standard registration		Internal audits 100% to plan, throughout year
	Resources	• Great place to work	Establish flexible/adaptable working arrangements	New contracts of employment agreed by Nov 2016
		• Reward people for quality and speed up, and cost down	Incentive objectives relate to top objectives	New appraisals system 100% completed by April 2016
			Survey people satisfaction and retention	Annual staff survey. Satisfaction >95% by Jan 2017
		• Enhance potential of resources for creating value-added, including facilities and people competencies	Machines development	5% output improvement – e.g. from speed and uptime. 10% variability reduction – e.g. from deviance to tolerances.
		• Comply with H&S	Conforming H&S risk assessment	Effective response to H&S committee actions, throughout year

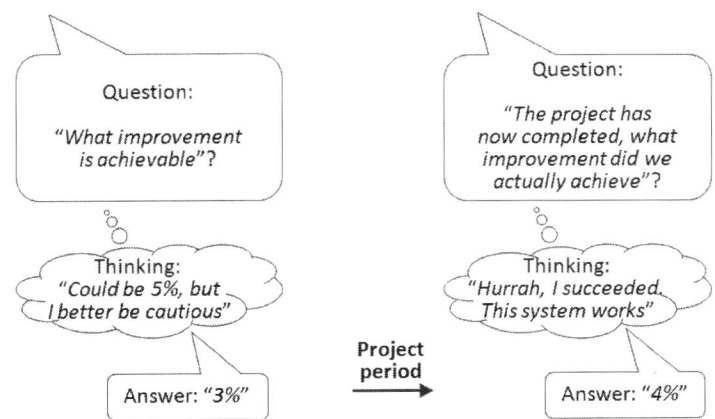

Cautious approach to setting a target.

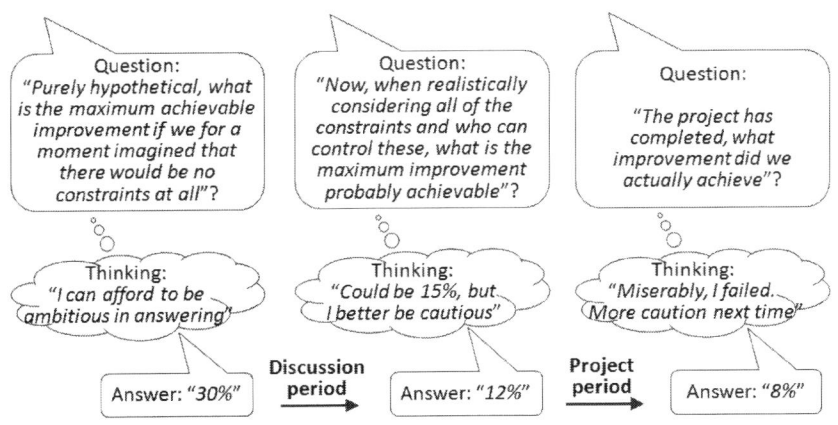

Stretch approach to setting a target

SETTING TARGETS

As rule of thumb, for most systems, there is nearly always 30% improvement to be foreseeably gained, under ideal perfect conditions. And, if the 30% where to be realised then there is nearly always further 30% improvement to be found in the remainder and so on. The trouble is that organisations rarely operate under ideal conditions and with perfect foresight. There are invariably constraints on an organisation, which make it practically impossible to straightforwardly see and reach the 30% target. Although some of these constraints may be deemed to be outside the organisations control, most tend in fact to be within its control – if it just pulled itself together and accepted that it must find and do something about them.

The setting of targets can become influenced by human behavioural factors, namely the fear of failure. Depending on the organisation's tolerance of failures, those responsible and accountable for the targets can select either a cautious or a stretch approach to setting them. A management system controlled by a blame and shame culture will naturally foster the cautious approach, because people would want to avoid failure at any cost. By contrast, a management system operating the stretch approach will show tolerance of, admissible, shortfalls in meeting the higher targets. Although the stretch approach tends to produce better results, it can unfairly reduce people's sense of success. Those accountable for the targets will therefore still apply some degree of caution. Shaming people for not reaching a stretch target will result in a drift towards the cautious approach in future targets setting, and an overall reduction in outcomes can follow. It is therefore important to put the relative 'under-achievement' against a stretch target into perspective, and to highlight and celebrate the positives in the result. There is no shame in not meeting a stretch target. There is only shame in not having tried to stretch in the first place.

OPERATION AND SUPPORT

Operation and support are basically everything that it takes to transform all the input requirements into an output.

OPERATION

Operation encompasses all the processes necessary for bringing the product, or service, into existence. 'Product' is defined as *"a tangible or intangible output that is the result of a process"*. Operational processes include, for example, product design, buying and stocking components parts, production, environmental protection, safety procedures, testing and inspecting, packing, promoting, selling, financial transacting, delivering, servicing, answering customer queries and, eventually, disposal if required. The operation shall be planned (see previous chapter).

The operational model may be prescribed in part by an external source, such as an industry standard or in law, or it may be defined by the organisation's own determination – i.e. what it has formulated in its policy, process maps, descriptive statements, drawings, specifications, instructions or whatever form is appropriate for the particular scenario. It is essential to have clear definitions for the operational processes, to enable the integrated management system objectively determining how effectively and efficiently the product was made – i.e. as a measure to gauge whether the planned process and outcome was met. Process definitions are also important in review and improvement of the operation, by providing a common understanding and perspective on what is going on across the organisation.

The following should be considered when planning and defining the operation:

- Objectives and requirements to be met.
- Resources allocation.
- Processes definitions and, if necessary, documentation.
- Output acceptance criteria, including how to be measured.
- Risks and opportunities.
- Records requirements.

SUPPORT

Support includes people, training, facilities, work environment, plant, equipment, measurement equipment, information, documentation, IT, communication, transportation and other resources. Support must be appropriate and sufficient for operating the processes. Just as the operational process itself, the supporting resources are continually developed.

PEOPLE

People are a particularly dynamic resource. Firstly, they are extremely flexible and adaptable, compared to a machine. Secondly, the individual person has an independent mind, which is sensitive to its environment. People's abilities, concentrations and commitments vary continually. People need to be equipped with the skills, knowledge, support and motivation necessary to perform their tasks well. People also need to be aware of the organisation's values and objectives, and understand how their own individual function contributes to meeting these.

FACILITIES

Facilities include infrastructure, such as building, equipment, IT and telephony, and the associated work environment. The work environment refers to the physical, social and psychological conditions – such as temperature, lighting, ergonomics, recognition schemes and occupational stresses. These factors will affect how work is performed and the outcomes. In certain industries, such as retail and restaurants for example, the facility and its environment, or ambiance, are key elements of the customer experience and effectively become part of the product. Location factors such as distance to suppliers and customers, employees supply, and sufficient space for facility expansion can also impact on outcomes.

Documentation in Processes

The integrated management system should document any element of the operation that can affect the effective planning, operation and control of its processes and information. The extent to this requirement is reflected in the external standards adopted by the organisation, which will typically specify that particular documentation and records be adequately established.

The processes in an improving organisation are likely to periodically change. Information knowledge about the needs of customers and other interested parties will also continually change. It is therefore important to establish a system for assuring that we are working to the currently correct processes and information. If we were to work to the incorrect information, then the operation will likely produce a product that does not conform to the requirements. It could make the difference in complying with the latest safety regulation, for example.

Documents are liable to be updated by their internal or external owners. The management system should therefore have a process in place for controlling and monitoring the correct use of all the documents and records that can influence the outcome from its operation. Documents should be readily available at point of use. They should be retained and preserved, until no longer required, as evidence of conformity and to provide confidence that processes are being carried out as planned.

PERFORMANCE EVALUATION

On the simplest level, performance evaluation is about monitoring that plans and requirements are satisfactorily met. On a better level, it further provides learning about risk mitigation and improvement opportunities.

Performance evaluation involves measuring, investigating, verifying, analysing and reviewing the planned arrangements and their outcomes. The earlier chapter on Planning describes how to determine the planned arrangements – i.e. how to get from what we want to a corresponding result. Customer outcome and management system effectiveness should practically always be part of the planned performance evaluation arrangement.

MEASUREMENT

The performance evaluation system element includes measuring the operational processes, at appropriate stages and intervals, in accordance with the planned arrangements and for maintaining evidence of conformity. This includes measurement and evaluation of suppliers who are essential to the planned outcome.

Measurements should be recorded and indicate who and how the measurement was made – for example, who authorised the release of the product as being fit for purpose. The measurement process should also define how to control and what to do with any product that does not meet the planned criteria.

The measurement system, such as test equipment and inspectors, should be verified and maintained to ensure it continually remains suitable for the monitoring and measurement activity it performs. When traceability is a requirement or if it is considered essential to providing confidence in the product being fit for purpose, the measurement equipment must be periodically calibrated against an assured standard and protected from deterioration in accuracy. If a calibration check proves the measurement equipment unfit for its intended purpose then the validity of its previous measurements should be re-considered.

AUDITING

Auditing is a systematic process for obtaining and evaluating evidence, against a reference model that contains a set of pre-defined criteria. The purpose of auditing is to:

- Measure effectiveness in meeting objectives.
- Verify conformance to stated requirements.
- Identify opportunities for improvement.

First-party auditing is an internal process conducted by trained employees, for the organisation's own purposes.

Second-party auditing is conducted by customers of the organisation, or by a customer representative.

Third-party auditing is conducted by an external independent body, usually accredited to provide certification of conformity.

The organisation will establish an audit plan, based on the status and importance of the individual processes. The plan defines intervals, scope, audit criteria and methods to be used. The criteria are the requirements or expectations that are stated in policies, procedures, or in customer, company and legal documents within the scope of the audit. The criteria are used as a reference against which the audit evidence is compared. Audit evidence encompasses records, statements or other factual information which are relevant to the audit criteria and are verifiable. The audit findings are recorded and translated into appropriate corrective and preventive actions, in agreement with the management responsible for the area under review. The actions should be followed-up, to verify that planned outcomes are achieved, before formally closing the audit.

SELF-CHECKS

A tool for the periodic systematic examination of a work area, for purpose of finding example evidence that requirements in company standards and work instructions are continuously met. This helps reduce the risk of mistakes and deviance from a defined process. The self-check is an opportunity for a team leader to review and identify issues in an activity. It can thereby support corrections and improvement.

Item			
Description:	Complete item / Sub-part of bigger item		
Traceable reference to the sample reviewed			
How much of the team's work time/emphasis is spent on this kind of work item			%
All people working on the item have received appropriate and sufficient training		Yes	No
Sample viewed is worked correctly, considering the process and any work instruction		Yes	No
Quality of completion of sample viewed is acceptable, considering customer viewpoint		Yes	No
Speed of completion is acceptable, considering customer and company viewpoint		Yes	No
Work documents are adequate to assure a trained person can complete correctly		Yes	No
Any work document or instruction is followed correctly		Yes	No

Example self-check list. The Appendix provides a fuller example of a practical form.

Self-checks are not truly independent, as per the definition of auditing. However, completed self-checks can be sampled by an independent auditor, to validate and give credibility to their objectiveness and thereby help simplify the internal auditing process. The self-check process makes team leaders understand and appreciate the process and value of auditing, thereby making the independent auditing processes more effective.

Management review

The review is a regular planned component of the organisation's performance evaluation activities. Not all elements of a management system are necessarily evaluated at every management review, but the various aspects should be on a schedule that addresses all the organisations planned objectives and processes over an appropriate cycle. The inputs and outputs of the management review should be recorded.

Inputs

The inputs cover all subject areas within the Integrated Management System. In-depth reviews of specific subject areas can be conducted by a sub-team, reporting back a summarised result and for the endorsement of any recommended actions by the whole management review team. Example input topics:

- Financials.
- Efficiency.
- Risks, opportunities.
- Resources.
- Quality.
- Environmental.
- Energy consumption.
- Health and safety.
- Complaints, accidents and failures summary/analysis.
- Audit results.
- Status of ongoing corrective measures.

Outputs

Defined actions for correcting or improving:

- Systems and processes.
- Products, including services.
- Resources.
- Organisational objectives.

IMPROVEMENT

Improvement is "a*n activity to increase the ability to fulfil requirements*", with aim to "*increase the probability of the system enhancing satisfaction with outcomes*".

The organisation's effective and timely fulfilment of its planned objectives is reliant on the ongoing performance evaluation and management reviews. Improvements can be made to the integration and the effectiveness of the management system, or they can be made to products and services.

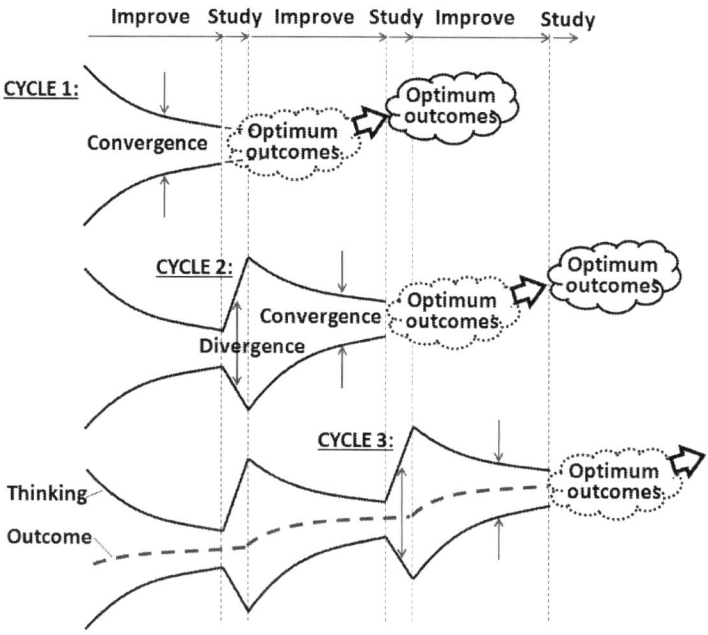

Map of thinking modes and how they affect outcomes.

The map of thinking modes represents cycles that are based on the general principles of moving between divergent and convergent modes of thinking. Divergent thinking refers to open minded study of what is expected of the organisation. The convergence phase will subsequently select some key measures and work more control-centrically on homing in on the target outcomes. Having perfected the measures that were defined in a previous study is no guarantee that we have optimised the outcomes, because we are in fact chasing a dynamic target. The 'Optimum outcomes' would have moved on, while we were homing in on the previously defined standard and, in the process, we have merely become really good at doing something that there now is a lesser need for. It is then time to study the requirements afresh and redefine the next new target measures, to track the moving 'Optimum outcomes'. The absolute optimum is an elusive notion that continually changes in form and is practically impossible to ever perfect. Organisations succeed by tracking the optimum as closely as possible.

In the study phase the focus is primarily qualitative. The study phase finishes by translating the newly defined qualitative requirements into quantitative measures – i.e. KPIs – which represents the system's new targets. The subsequent improvement phase has more of a quantitative focus – i.e. it is about homing onto the measurable KPI targets. We must work both qualitatively and quantitatively in this way. The faster we can improve, and hence the more study phases we can efficiently fit in, the closer a distance to the 'Optimum outcomes' can be maintained. We cannot study indefinitely, however, because the study itself does not get any improvement work done. The divergent thinking of the study phase can momentarily take us off course. Once the study is done and we have decided on the requirements to focus on, then we converge onto the redefined 'Optimum outcomes'. Each cycle demands an investment in time. The frequency of cycles can be too high, resulting in a loss of continuity and giving insufficient time for improvements to be established. You may have heard of the term 'initiatives overload'. **The best result is achieved by an effective study, followed by a period where a high rate of improvement is achieved. When the rate of improvement slows then it signals that a new study may be beneficial.**

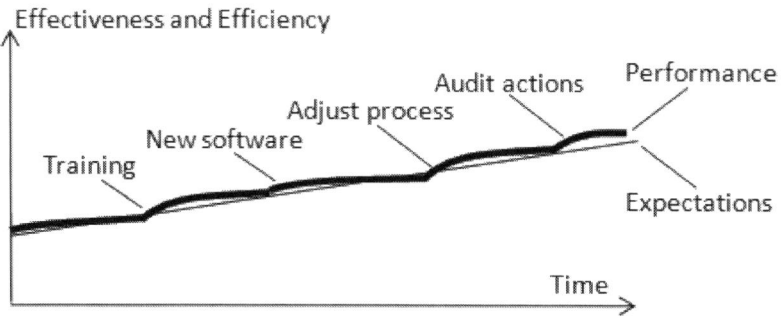

Improving performance versus raising expectations.

EVIDENCE-BASED DECISION MAKING

Decision making is the forming of a causal argument that a chosen alternative will result a particular future outcome. The quality of a decision is largely dependent on the accuracy and relevance of the information on which it is based – as well as being free from subjective bias in reflecting the true needs. When poor quality or biased evidence is used for decision making, the proposed alternative will risk producing an ineffective or adverse outcome.

Evidence-based decision making is about establishing high level confidence in the causal argument's prediction of the future outcome. This is achieved by establishing relevant and sufficiently accurate information to support the choice being made. Well-defined processes and well-trained people equipped with effective, cost-efficient data collection and analysis devices will improve the organisations decision making competence. Good decision evidence also ensures transparency and accountability. When presented with the same evidence, anyone looking at a situation should practically reach the same conclusion. The evidence effectively makes the decision.

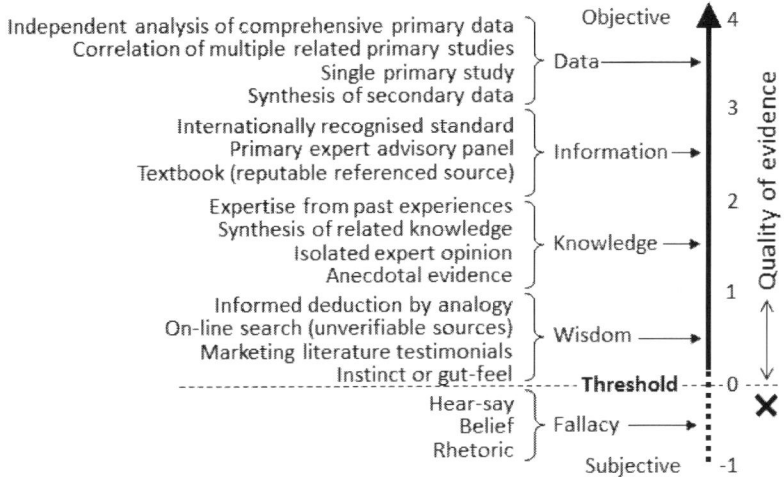

Hierarchy of evidence-base [adapted from DIKW pyramid]

The term 'primary data' defines what was collected for the specific purpose of the immediate study. 'Secondary data' was collected for some other purpose, but is considered transferable to the new purpose. Primary data tends to be more relevant and thereby improve predictability in the causal argument.

In practice, the evidence will consist of some data, some information, some knowledge and some wisdom, producing a total level of quality. When faced with a decision, think about where the evidence-base is on the quality scale and think about where it should ideally be, to provide sufficient confidence in the decision. If the main source of evidence cannot establish the full extent of required confidence – say, if only a partial data set is obtainable – then supplement with other sources of evidence. The multiple sources will complement each other and add up to an overall level of quality. When multiple sources of partial confidence evidence agree, then it adds strength to the overall quality of evidence. Similarly, say, if two sets of data are in conflict then it weakens the overall quality of evidence.

We must be pragmatic when determining the sufficiency in the quality of evidence. Moving from unreliable subjective information to reliable objective data in the hierarchy of the evidence-base will improve the predictive powers of a decision, but it will also demand an increased investment in information resources and time. Sufficiency must appropriately balance the opportunities from making a good decision with the risks from making a poor decision, including consideration to any urgency demanded from the immediate situation. Intuition and gut-feel is rarely reliable in reaching optimum decisions; but under certain urgent circumstances their method may be necessary, to counter an adverse risk associated with a delayed decision. When circumstances force the reliance of less than ideal evidence, then establish monitoring steps to help the earliest possible detection of a sub-optimal decision and to enable a timely corrective action.

ANALYSIS

Good analysis is essential to effective problem-solving and decision making. Analysis is a systematic detailed examination and evaluation of the parts or data from a situation, for purpose of uncovering how they relate to each other. Analysis is often used to help defining causes and effects, through different types of reasoning:

Heuristic: Based on trial and error learning, common sense, rule of thumb, or educated guessing.

Inductive: Establishment of directly relevant and undisputable evidential arguments for the truth.

Deductive: Establishment of logical transferable arguments that says if something is true in one context then it is safe to conclude it is equally true in an analogous second context.

Analysis is often based on multiple sources and types of evidenced-based information, some of which can be subjective (see previous section on Evidence-based decision making).

PROACTIVE AND REACTIVE ACTIONS

Prevention is about predicting and proactively eliminating the causes of potential failures <u>before</u> they can occur. The preventive action process involves measurement and analysis, to determine the appropriate risks mitigation and opportunities for eliminating the potential failure root causes. Statistical measurement and analysis are particularly important in predicting potentially adverse trends. Failure Mode Effect Analysis (FMEA) is another important prevention tool (see in later section). If it is important to the conformity assurance system, the preventive action should be recorded for evidence.

Corrections are reactively made <u>after</u> the planned results were not being achieved, including on receiving a customer complaint or discovering an internal process failure. The corrective action consists of an investigation, analysis and improvement, to eliminate the root cause and prevent a re-occurrence. The action should be proportionate to the situation. Actions should be reviewed to verify their effectiveness, following implementation, and to determine whether further action is needed. Reactive corrective actions should be recorded, for learning and for evidence that the organisation is serious about achieving conformance to requirements.

SUPPLIERS

Even if they are not part of the organisation itself, those suppliers who have a significant influence on the final product to customers should be considered similarly as if they are part of the organisation's system. In fact, in some sectors, a supplier can have a greater influence on outcomes than the organisation's own resources have. A well-managed supply chain is important to the stable flow of the operation. In our model, we have referred to suppliers as being an 'external' element of the integrated management system. As for all other elements of the system, the organisation would want its suppliers to continually improve. Nearly all sectors experience cycles of change and economic pressures. The supply-chain should share this pressure with a degree of equity. Just keeping on pushing the pressure up the supply-chain will result in a skewed relationship, where one party sets all the conditions and reap all the rewards. This may not be a recipe for long-term success (unless it helps unsettling a stifling supply-chain stagnation). The unfairly subordinated party is unlikely to invest his best effort in such a relationship.

There are no hard and fast rules when it comes to deciding what activities to outsource to suppliers and what activities to keep in-house. Generally, core activities where the organisation's management and people talents have most effect on outcomes – i.e. its special or unique value-generating competencies – should probably be maintained and developed in-house. Activities that add little value and which could just as well be done by anyone else may be better outsourced to a supplier, to prevent them from detracting focus and talent from the more important activities.

The success of supplier relationships depends on:

1. Finding the right supplier, with a 'matching' value view.
2. Be clear about what the organisation wants from its supplier.
3. Understand sensitivity to quantities and time commitment.
4. Negotiate for mutually benefits.
5. Monitor and manage relationship performance.

The right supplier shares the organisation's value (quality-price) strategy – e.g. has either an economy or premium product focus. The aim is to avoid buying too little quality or paying excess for needless quality.

The transfer price and cost are the two single most important matters for a commercial supplier. Nearly everything that a supplier does evolves around estimating them right and optimising their difference, without losing the customer. Suppliers know that the margin in the price they quote is not necessarily the one that they will finally obtain. Suppliers must factor-in perceivable risks to the final obtainable margin. Buyers invariably end-up paying for this risk, in one form or another. The organisation should therefore help mitigate the supplier's risks. Straightforward customers, who know what they want and pay on time, are perceived as low risk. Making a reliable commitment to quantities and time agreement will help the supplier to better plan and further reduce his risk-factors.

Monitor the relationships with suppliers as part of the management system's 'performance evaluation' activities. Think about how your processes can adversely impact on your suppliers, but demand the same consideration in return. Know where the organisation can be flexible on the features in what is supplied to it. Negotiate fairly, with equity. However, do not tolerate unreasonably poor quality or skewed high pricing. Replace poor suppliers, or seek to adopt an alternative solution to fulfilling your needs – ideally before things start going wrong.

CUSTOMERS AND INTERESTED PARTIES

Commercial and non-commercial organisations are established and exist to provide value to customers, for which the organisation receives an economic compensation in return. This exchange is essential for the organisation sustaining itself, to maintain the repeating cycle of providing value. Without the longer term continual ability to produce value to customers, there would be no basis for an organisation's existence.

Interested parties include the organisation owner, customer representative groups, society standards and regulatory bodies – basically anyone with a true interest in the performance or success of the organisation. The sustainability of an organisation is supported by well-managed relationships with its interested parties. The organisation should therefore determine the relevance of all individual interested parties and appropriately engage with or otherwise monitor their requirements, needs and perceived opinions.

CUSTOMER NEEDS

A well-defined 'Voice of Customer' (VOC) is in some respect the most important, but simultaneously a difficult research activity to get absolutely right for an organisation. It is about understanding and clearly defining what customers need and what they want, and also what they could tolerate less of and what they do not want at all. Expectations are forever increasing, and yesterday's standard will always lack behind current capability and needs.

Do not simply focus on the first expressed needs. Explore what customers think and experience, and why. This helps to identify the strengths of customer demands and what excites them the most. There will be many different views and priorities on what the customer needs. Remember, the silent majority of customers can be more important than the vocal minority. We therefore must quantify and produce statistics relating to the strengths and the proportions of customers who need something.

The term 'need' could be wrong in some context. Customers tend to express their 'wants', and are often not aware of or ambitious enough about their needs. They can possess a short horizon-span, where they see their needs mainly in relation to products they already know. If we are to excite customers towards our product or service, then we must find opportunities for answering needs that are not yet fully realised or addressed – in effect turning needs into new wants. However, be mindful of not selecting something we think customers need, but that is too alien in concept and they are not yet ready for. The success in convincing the customer is based on a degree of trust, where stronger brands will find it easier to lead customers to accept new solutions.

Customer Satisfaction

Noriaki Kano developed a model for classifying customer needs into three categories, each of which influencing satisfaction in a different way. Importantly, the model tells that the prevention of wrong-doing is not the same as doing right. **A strategy based solely on removing dissatisfaction can over time never result in satisfied customers**. The model thereby highlights a dilemma with traditional quality assurance, seeking to control everything to pre-defined standards. Yesterday's standard will always lack behind current capability and needs. Sustained success depends on continually exceeding and evolving the standards and expectations.

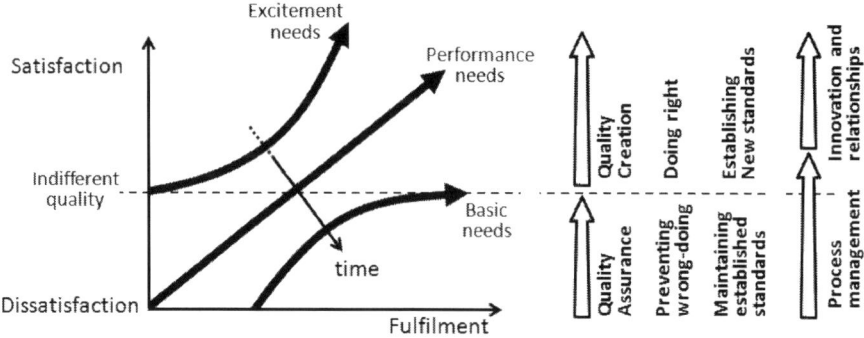

Kano diagram (adapted) indicating various contributors to customer satisfaction.

Kano model definitions	
Indifferent quality	Neutral value level, where customer is neither satisfied, nor dissatisfied.
Basic needs	Something taken for granted when present – meaning they are not necessarily asked for and they do not add satisfaction. However, their non-fulfilment will result in dissatisfaction. Also referred to as threshold needs or must-be requirements, because the customer might reject the product or service if they are not met. The fulfilment of basic needs is therefore a prerequisite for the performance and excitement needs being accepted. A customer's affordability threshold can be thought of as a basic need, and sometimes demands a trade-off.
Performance needs	Attributes or features that customers ask for and against which they intent to measure their buying decision. The more the product or service promises to fulfil this need the more the customer is satisfied with making the buying/using choice.
Excitement needs	Emotional engagement or reaction. Makes a pleasant surprise when encountered. Will not be missed if omitted, because customers have not yet realised that they want it. However, omission is a lost opportunity for high satisfaction and for gaining new customers.
Time	Any excitement effect is only temporary. The novelty-value eventually wears off and the feature becomes considered as the norm. Over time it turns into a performance need, and can eventually turn basic.

Further definitions	
Quality Assurance	Prevention of wrong-doing, by managing activities to known standards.
Quality Creation	Doing right, in establishing new standards.
Innovation	Adds novelty excitement, stimulating an impulsive emotive desire. Feeds the customer's self-esteem from being recognised as trendy. Lifts performance and/or reduces costs to new levels.
Relationships	Emotional engagement, which adds strength of personal attachment or a kind of shared ownership bond, making the customer's view more favourable towards the organisation's product.
Process management	Ensures that pre-existing requirements are identified and that things are done correctly. Provides a stable platform to improve and innovate from.

Quality practitioners now-a-days tend to treat the term "quality assurance" as being too narrow for purpose. They prefer instead to talk about "quality management" or "quality systems". History shows that over-emphasis on the term "assurance" can drive a limited kind of quality, which would not necessarily guarantee satisfaction. Innovation and relationships can be effectively achieved within systematic processes. The most successful innovators are in fact process-driven. Process management does not in itself excite customers, but it assures that pre-existing requirements are identified and that things are done correctly. It must not hinder the freedom to be innovative and to attach a 'personal touch' in building emotionally engaging customer relationships. Process management effectively provides the essential prerequisite stable platform, from which to deliver and improve customer satisfaction.

In a purely utility view of quality – i.e. fitness for purpose, at best price – we may only need to consider the basic needs. Customers for commodity products, such as electricity and gas supply services for example, are less influenced by excitement needs. Although saying that, relationships still matters. Most people switch utility service provider not because of the price or a bad product, but only when something goes wrong in their personal relationship with the provider's customer services.

WHAT LEVEL OF DISSATISFACTION WILL PEOPLE TOLERATE?

Ideally, quality is naturally inherent in the product, in a way that dissatisfaction is simply never an issue. In the real world, however, organisations and their operating environments are dynamically complex. Everything that interacts has variability. The provision of a product or service will rely on hundreds, if not thousands, of small interactions where unintended variability can creep in. It is utopian thinking that poor quality can never happen. At best, we can maintain variability at such a low level where our customer can easily tolerate the trivial/minor flaws.

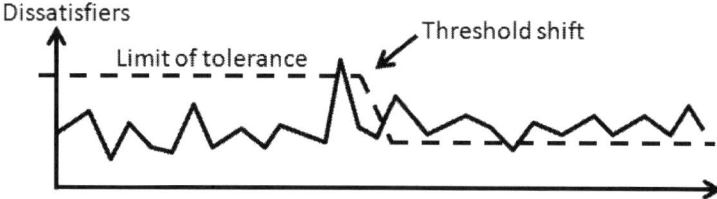

Shift in the customer's limit of tolerance to dissatisfiers.

The relationship between quality and satisfaction is not a linear one. There can be a fine line between 'everything good' and 'everything bad'. While customers overall are satisfied and while they like the organisation's people or brand, it can feel as if the organisation can do nothing wrong. Customers can tolerate a degree of the odd dissatisfier. However, as soon as the limit of tolerance is exceeded and dissatisfaction is triggered, then everything – even the slightest deviance – becomes perceived as bad. The limit of tolerance is thereby dynamic. As soon as the organisation just once peaks above the threshold, the tolerance can suddenly shift downwards to reveal a multitude of issues that no-one realised matter much. The rate of threshold recovery is slower and can become trapped in a self-perpetuating downwards spiral of dissatisfaction. Customers who abandon an organisation will usually only come back following a poor experience with the alternative provider organisation that they sought to use. Staying clear of the limit of tolerance threshold will therefore tend to naturally increase customer numbers over time. Taking risks in playing it too close to the limit of tolerance, and misjudging it, can have a potentially catastrophic effect.

Note: The exact same tolerance threshold graph holds true for employee satisfaction. In kind of a similar way, an organisation is under a constant risk of switching off its employees. If this happens then it can result in a significant loss of the organisation's performance and output, which it will take time to recover.

Standards

A standard is a recognised norm or model defining requirements or an acceptable level of attainment, and which can be used for qualitative or quantitative comparison to an actual situation. A standard can also be a technical specification, protocol and/or nomenclature for use in establishing compatibility between systems. The extent of recognition of a standard varies between:

- International standard, adopted across the world.
- Transnational standard, covering a number of countries.
- National standard, covering a single country – although sometime recognised by customers and authorities in other countries (i.e. it can be practically transnational).
- Independent standard, subscribed to by members of a society, an association, scheme or particular industry that may span nationally or internationally.

Mostly, an International standard tend to be adopted and evolved from an original National or Transnational standard, which itself may have originated in an Independent standard. This process also operates in reverse, with National standards organisations adopting International standards for national purposes.

New standards are collaboratively evolved in a consensus-based process involving all of the members of the standard organisation. This can be a long process. New standards are many years in the making and the first versions tend to be either too openly compromising or too narrowly scoped in their application. Established standards continue to be periodically reviewed and revised, as necessary to keep up with changing norms and application. The ISO 9001 quality management standard, for example, has changed and evolved for over 50 years. Its early forerunner was developed as an independent standard in the American defence industry in early 1960's, from where a revised family of standards was 'transnationalised' across to European NATO countries. The standard was subsequently reshaped for commercial application, initially, in the 1970's, as BS 9000 on quality in the electronic components industry. This standard was revised for general manufacturing quality assurance in the 1980's. In the 1990's the standard was made furthermore generic, including variants for the service and the measurement industries. The year 2000 revision further broadened the standard with the concept of a generic process management approach, thereby evolving beyond its legacy control-centric assurance focus. The 2008 revision could finally be said to be workable for (nearly) all industries. The standard is still evolving, with the 2015 version yet again revising the system model and enhancing the elements of managing risks and opportunities.

The International Standards Organisation (ISO) is probably the most recognisable and most broad-reaching of its kind today. It was formed in 1946 *"to facilitate the international coordination and unification of industrial standards"*. The ISO has forerunners, many of which are still relevant today. Of these, the International Electrotechnical Commission (IEC) was founded in 1906. Some of the independent standards societies today, such as Underwriters Laboratories (now UL), can trace their roots back even earlier.

MANAGEMENT SYSTEM STANDARDS

For those organisations that formally adopt more than one management systems standard, they will today find that the standards increasingly align and correspond to each other in their fundamental concept and layout. This is because the ISO is now aligning all new management standard revisions to a common

High Level Structure (HLS) and shared core language. The HLS is built on the Plan-Do-Check-Act cycle and incorporates risk-based thinking. The HLS specifies the following 10 standard headings, each defining a varied mix of sub-clauses:

1. Scope
2. Normative references
3. Terms and definitions
4. Context of the organization
5. Leadership
6. Planning
7. Support
8. Operation
9. Performance evaluation
10. Improvement

ISO 9001

International standard on requirements for a quality management system, where an organisation needs to demonstrate its ability to consistently meet customer and regulatory requirements; and where it aims to enhance customer satisfaction through improvement.

The quality system standard is based on a generic process approach and simply defines product as the *"result of a process"*. This makes it universally applicable to any type of organisation, regardless of size and product or service provided. In practice, the ISO 9001 standard is a set of descriptive requirements for what is universally recognised should be contained in a management system that effectively seeks to achieve and continually enhance quality. It does not prescribe how these requirements shall be met. It is for the organisation self to determine how it will meet them, in a way that best suits its particular situation. By nature of its product, an organisation can exclude itself from some of the requirements – as long as this does not affect the ability or responsibility towards the customer, statutory and regulatory requirements. The organisation determines and, for clarity, documents the scope of its quality management system – i.e. what processes and products are covered by the ISO 9001 conforming system – and considers the justification for those that it feel it does not need to include.

ISO 9001 belongs to a family of standards, including ISO 9000 on quality fundamentals and vocabulary; and the ISO 9004 guidance standard on a quality approach to managing for the sustained success of an organisation. The family of standards centres on seven quality management principles, which are:

1. Customer focus.
2. Leadership.
3. Engagement of people.
4. Process approach.
5. Improvement.
6. Evidence-based decision making.
7. Relationship management.

ISO 9001 has several sector specific variants – for example:

> ISO 18091 on *"guidelines for the application of ISO 9001 in local government"* – a sector specific guidance standard, which does not add, change or modify any of the requirements at all.

> ISO 13485 on *"medical devices quality management system"* – a sector specific variant that supplements with a small number of additional requirements, to facilitate 'harmonization' with transnational medical device regulations (to support the free movement of goods across more geographical regions).

Often stated benefits from adopting ISO 9001 have included:

- Increased customer confidence and satisfaction potential.

- Strengthened platform for innovation and improvement.
- Assured future viability and existence, by maintaining relevance to evolving customer needs and addressing risks and opportunities.
- Wider market access, by ability to demonstrate conformity to regulatory requirements.
- Reduced likelihood of civil and criminal litigation.
- Competitive advantages, from customer confidence.
- Self-esteem and recognition.
- Reduced burden of inspection, in contract services. One periodic third-party assessment, instead of multiple lesser coordinated client audits.
- Cost saving potential, from less failures and remedial work.

ISO 14001

International standard on requirements for an environmental management system, where an organisation needs to demonstrate its ability to meet regulatory requirements, and/or where it aims to reduce waste.

It is increasingly important to demonstrate that organisations are thinking about their environmental impact and have put in place systems that will not only assure compliance with environmental protection regulations, but will also improve efficiency and reduce costs with regards to its environmental management.

Often stated benefits from adopting ISO 14001 have included:

- Assured future viability and existence, by addressing risks and opportunities in operating sustainably.
- Wider market access, by ability to demonstrate conformity to global environmental requirements.
- Reduced likelihood of environmental prosecution.
- Competitive advantages, from reputation.

- Self-esteem and recognition.
- Reduced or more flexible regulatory inspections for obtaining operating permits.
- Cost saving potential, from resources consumption, waste, recycling and lower insurance premium.

ISO 50001/EN 16001

Internationally adopted European transnational standard on requirements for an energy management system, where an organisation aims to reduce energy use and/or needs to demonstrate its ability to meet regulatory requirements for energy use.

ISO 50001 (international) and EN 16001 (European version) requirements incorporate guidelines for meeting regulatory carbon emissions targets, through the establishment of an energy policy with firm objectives and planned actions for monitoring and reducing energy use, and for verifying energy outcomes and improvement.

Often stated benefits from adopting ISO 50001/EN 16001 have included:

- Assured future viability and existence, by improved management of energy risk and regulatory requirements.
- Wider market access, by ability to demonstrate conformity to global greenhouse-gas and carbon footprint requirements, many of which are evolving from being voluntary to increasingly becoming mandatory and enforced.
- Reduced likelihood of prosecution.
- Competitive advantages, from protection of credibility.
- Self-esteem and recognition.

- Cost saving potential, from a managed approach to continually reducing energy consumption and avoidance of fines.

OHSAS 18001

Internationally applied British standard (is for example published in Spanish, Russian, Chinese) on requirements for an occupational health and safety management system, where an organisation needs to demonstrate sound occupational health and safety performance, to aid legal compliance, and aims to improve overall health and safety.

At time of writing, the national standard is in its final stage of being adopted internationally as ISO 45001.

Often stated benefits from adopting OHSAS 18001 have included:

- Ability to demonstrate conformity to health and safety laws.
- Reduced likelihood of civil litigation and criminal prosecution.
- Competitive advantages, from providing a safe customer environment – e.g. where the organisation invites and serves its customers on its own premises.
- Employee morale and satisfaction, from experiencing a safer working environment.
- Cost saving potential, from minimised disruptions from accidents and lower public liability insurance premium.

Integrated Processes Documentation

This section is an illustrative example for demonstrating the concept of implementing integration in processes documentation. Formal management standards, such as ISO 9001, do in fact not prescribe any particular structure for this.

The integrated management system should define, and document when appropriate, any process that can affect the effective planning, operation and control of any of the system standards that the organisation has adopted. Do not define processes for trivial activities or those that professional people are trained to know how to perform – unless the absence of a defined process could potentially result in a real risk of an adverse deviance from the organisations objectives. Some legally required processes may have to be documented to reflect a certain specification – such as for Occupational Health & Safety.

For each individual process, all of the organisational, standard and regulatory requirements – from the various different sources – are combined into the single process definition, in a coherent way. For example, we do not create management review processes for each the quality system and the environmental system; but instead create a single process that reviews quality and environmental systems together, in one activity. A single overall process owner is defined, who is responsible for establishing and maintaining the criteria to be satisfied, and who all process operators are answering to. The multiple processes documentations are further combined into a single 'process manual' (or whatever you may choose to name it), as opposed to separate quality system and environmental system manuals.

As part of effective internal communication, it is good practice for the process manual defining the organisation's overall core process(es) in a single representation, recognisably incorporating all the key elements of the Integrated Management Model. This provides people with the understanding of the wider interrelationships, to enable them appreciate the contribution and impact from their own localised decision making.

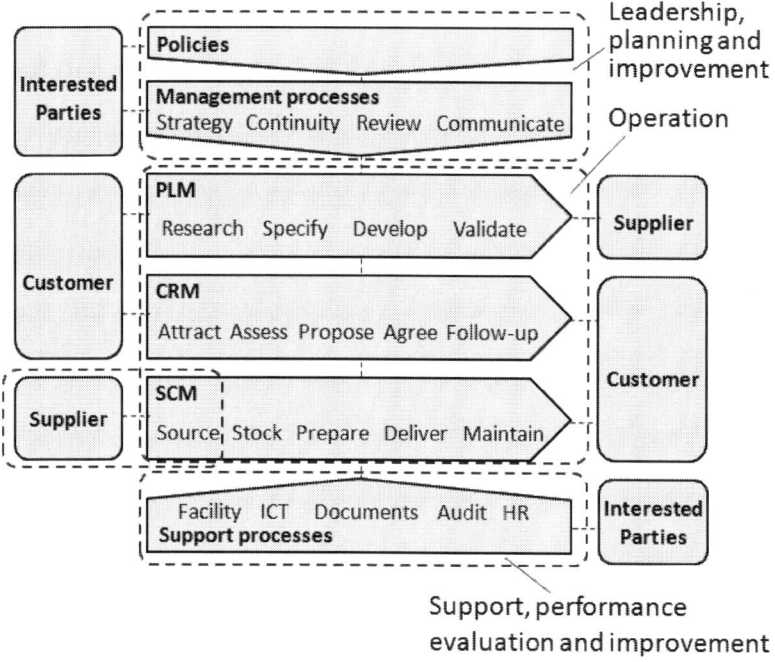

Example core processes map.

The example map of core processes, here above, relate to a degree to the standard management system model. The discontinued lines roughly indicate where the model elements reside. The example has 3 core operational processes: PLM (Product Lifecycle Management), CRM (Customer Relationship Management) and SCM (Supply-Chain Management), each grouping has a naturally flowing set of sub-processes.

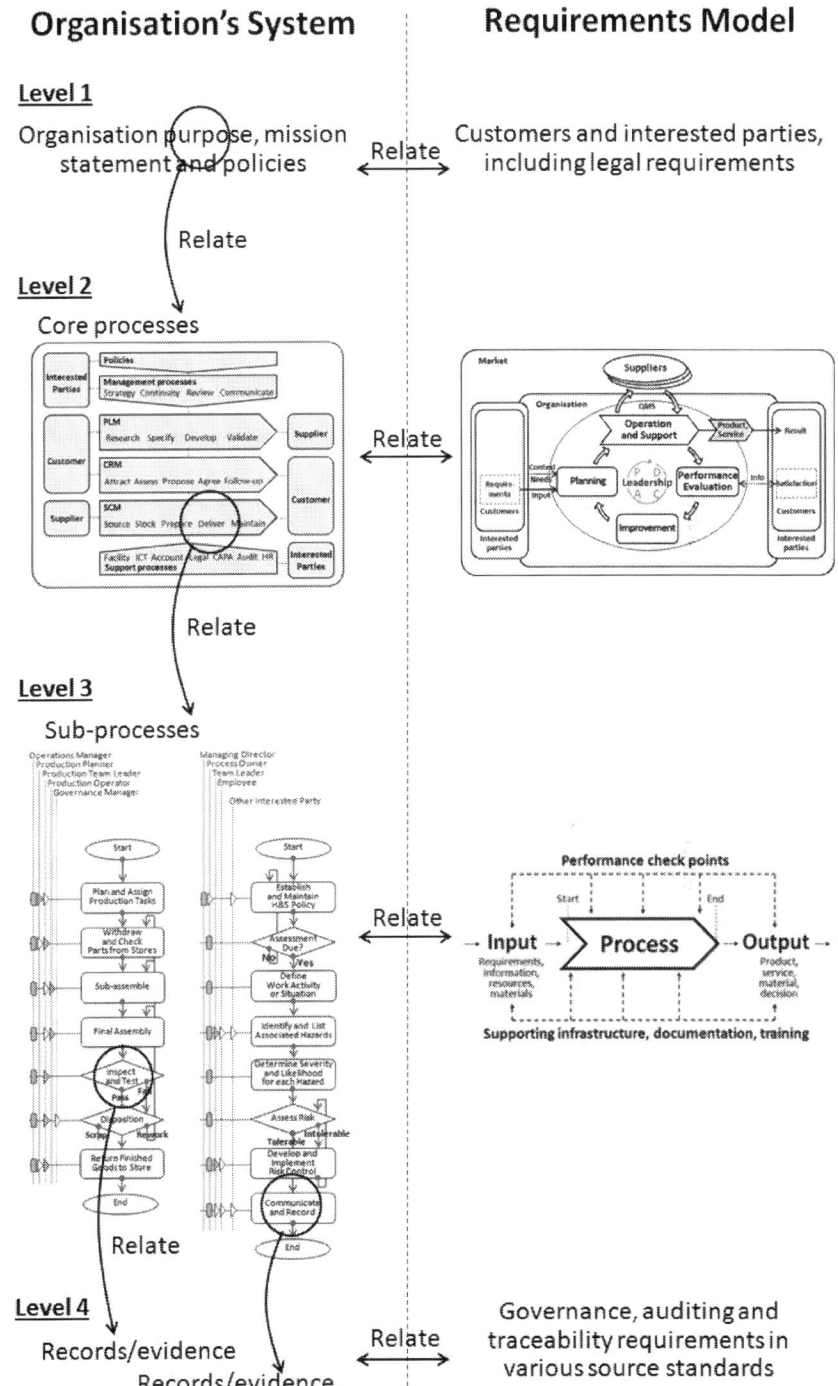

The integrated processes documentation has a hierarchical structure, which more or less reflects the cascading order in which they should be developed. For example, there is little point in defining the details of sub-processes, until the organisation's objectives and the core flow is clearly defined. The implementation of the management system model is governed by the organisation's strategy and policies, which may periodically change and thereby influence a rethink of the processes.

- Level 1   The organisation's purpose should relate to customer, interested parties and legal requirements.

- Level 2   The structure of core processes should relate to the Level 1 requirements and also incorporate the High-Level System model elements.

- Level 3   Individual processes and sub-processes should relate to the Level 2 structure and should also reflect the single process model.

- Level 4   Records and evidence produced from the system should meet requirements for governance, traceability and demonstrate a measurement of processes conformance/result.

The term 'governance' means "*the framework of rules and mechanisms for checks-and-balances, by which an organisation is overall directed and controlled*". Governance ensures that the organisation and its processes lawfully and fairly balance the interests of the many parties – including its owners, customers, finances and legal requirements.

Process design

By nature of changing needs, expectations and capabilities, and an organisation's need to continually satisfy its customers and interested parties, most processes are under-going continual incremental improvement. There will be times, however, where demands or conditions have changed so significantly that a more fundamental process re-design is required – beyond the mere incremental.

The following presents a simple approach to process design, or re-design. The approach may be expanded or refined with other tools and techniques.

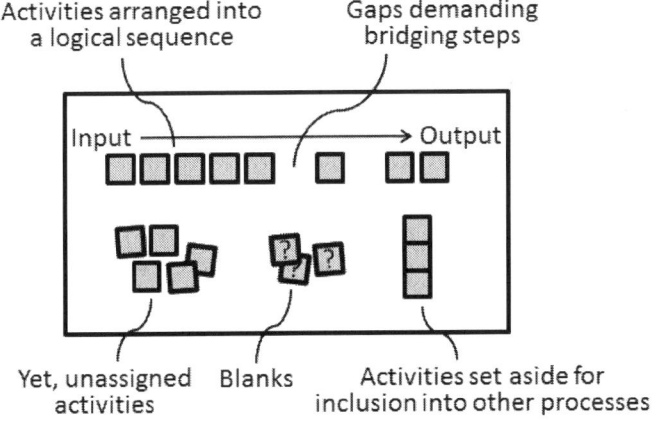

Functional activity cards being arranged into a logical sequence

Start by clarifying the needs of customers and interested parties. Determine what activities are required to deliver and satisfy those needs. Identify the risks and opportunities to be addressed. Record all of the activities, or tasks, to be performed onto cards or labels. The labels represent the tasks that the process must perform. In a group discussion, arrange the activities into a logical sequence, which makes sense, from the input to the final output of the process.

Apply best possible a set of guiding principles for process effectiveness and efficiency. Have some blank cards ready, because a new activity, or task, may be needed to bridge two steps, or if we may need to duplicate some (e.g. if data is recorded in several stages, and we initially only made one card for this), or if risk controls should need to be added. Consider also that some activities may have to transfer to specialist supporting or parallel processes (e.g. remote IT backup activity), where they – possibly – have a better or more economical fit. Document the final process, including its inputs, outputs, resources, methods and criteria for effectiveness, and its responsibility and authority. Compare and verify that it adequately relates to the single process model.

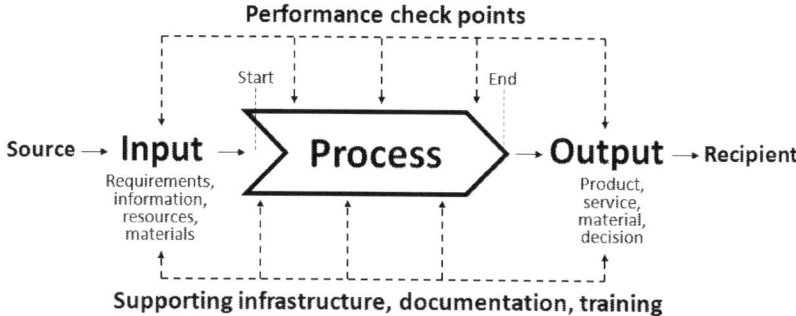

Single process model (adapted from ISO 9001:2015).

Guiding principles for process effectiveness and efficiency:

a) Avoid dividing a process into multiple specialised tasks. Instead, create 'case workers' or cross-functional self-steering 'case teams' for completing the full job. This reduces complexity of interfaces and eliminates the need for hand-offs, thereby increasing speed and responsiveness.

b) Directly connect the source and the user of something. This assures that the transfer between them is always complete and correct, to the user's requirement. This is sometimes referred to as 'end-to-end principle', which says that intermediaries (including managers/supervisors) introduce an uncontrollable degree of variability in a transfer. Where an intermediary is unavoidable (e.g. a goods courier or an information communication network), the two ends must have checks-and-balances in place to assure completeness and correctness in what is received at the user end.

c) Have those who use the output of a process also perform the process. This extends somewhat on points a) and b). For example, teams could make their own purchases, manage parts inventory, and carry out equipment maintenance. This eliminates the need for co-ordination and controlling functions (supervision), and reduces organisational barriers where one team must wait for others, who are not always readily available to come in to support.

d) Maximise capacity and skills for parallel processing, for increased speed and work flow flexibility. Flexible work units enable flow 'takt time' balancing for improved efficiency. For example, if step 1 takes 2 minutes to perform, and step 2 takes 1.5 minute to perform, then the capacity (operator or machine) at step 2 stands idle for 25% of the time. Ideally, we would want to move some of the work at step 1 to step 2, to balance the times to become equal. Coordinate the parallel activities, instead of blindly integrating their results. Late integration is a common cause of results mismatch and rework. The early linking facilitates a continual coordination.

e) Concentrate on the value-added. Reduce bureaucracy. Reduce non-value-adding support processes. For example, let operators perform their own preventive and corrective maintenance – instead of calling in a costly and difficult to schedule resource.

f) Capture information once, at source, to avoid re-entry work and its associated increase in error probability. Use robust data entry methods, such as barcodes or data tags. Merge information processing work into the real workflow that produces the information. People who collect information should also be responsible for processing it. They are more likely to recognise an error or abnormality.

g) Put decision points where the work is being performed. Recognise that the workforce can be trained and made knowledgeable. Open up for information transparency. It is in fact easy to provide teams with access to all the relevant information. This results in a more responsive organisation.

h) Maintain quality self-checks, as opposed to separate inspection functions. Build controls and mistake-proofing devices into the process, to prevent faults from being accepted into or travelling out from a process step. This raises personal responsibility and accountability.

i) Standardise processes and process equipment across the organisation, for reduced skills specialisation and greater flexibility.

RISK AND OPPORTUNITY

Although not truly the reciprocals of each other – because there can be opportunity without risk and vice versa – risk and opportunity must often be considered together.

Inability to exploit opportunity can present a risk.

Ability to control risk enables exploitation of opportunity.

It is bad – but not uncommon – when an organisation concedes: *"It would have been a fantastic thing to do; but just not right now because we currently have other issues to sort out first"*. Often, this is a perpetual excuse – because the unprepared organisation will always have other 'things' to resolve first. It is important to protect the capability and to maintain the resilience of resources in being able to address opportunities as they arise. Inaction, in a changing market, can prove the greatest risk of them all. Use risk-based thinking when developing and operating the Integrated Management System.

Risk-based thinking means to ensure that risks are identified, considered and controlled by a proactive approach. An opportunity is a set of circumstances that makes it possible to do something positive. Taking, or not taking, an opportunity presents varied levels of risk. Balancing risk and opportunity should be proportionate to their potential impact on the organisation and its outcomes. To put this in context of the Kano model that was presented earlier in this book, it is about controlling what can go wrong, while simultaneously maintaining or enhancing the capability for doing right. The approach to risk and opportunity is thereby said to have both defensive and offensive modes:

a) The defence mode is about establishing preventative and protective devices, to avoid failures or setbacks from unmanaged risks.

b) The offensive mode is about maintaining adaptability and scalability, to be readily poised to take advantage of new opportunities.

Addressing risk can include reducing or eliminating the probability of an adverse situation, or accepting and monitoring a tolerable amount of risk in order to pursue an opportunity.

Addressing opportunities can include taking on-board new practices, developing new products, opening new markets, reaching new customers or introducing new technology.

Importantly, risk management must not put the organisation into a straightjacket. When the organisation's wider operating environment, the market, is disrupted, the strongest and best prepared player can take advantage. Investments in resilience can give a business a competitive advantage over those who are not well prepared.

RISK MANAGEMENT

Risk management consists of processes to identify threats and vulnerabilities to the organisation, and then to define their appropriate countermeasures. Current management standards require a systematic approach to considering risks, and to planning and implementing their countermeasures. However, the standards do not specify any formal method for risk management.

Risks can be inter-dependent in a way that a balanced compromise has to be met. Sometimes risk management involves making an informed decision about accepting a particular level of risk, in order to reduce another more consequential risk – for example, in managing and optimally balancing the following risks:

> Risk register for a (hypothetical) new product development:
>
> Risk 1: Delay in launching the new product late, while the commercial window of opportunity is closing.
> Risk 2: Launching the product before it is ready and fully validated, potentially containing flaws.
> Risk 3: Exceeding the affordable project budget.

It is advisable to maintain a risk register, for both managing the individual risks and visualising the potentially conflicting risks. ISO 31000 provides a guidance standard (currently not for certification) on the principles, framework and process for managing risk. This standard may be a useful reference for organisations that need a more formal approach to risk management. The FMEA tool (see below) is another well-tested approach for registering and managing risks.

The organisation may have a risk management lead or co-ordinator, but such role is ideally not a separate function. The responsibilities for managing risks, and opportunities, should be dispersed throughout the integrated functions across the organisation.

FAILURE MODE AND EFFECTS ANALYSIS
A risk management tool for analysing potential failures and their effects on a system and for evaluating the development of countermeasure to prevent these effects from being realised.

Risk Analysis Worksheet

System	Organisation Name			Last review date	01/01/2016			
				Owner	Managing Director			

Severity: 1 = failure effect is negligible (no harm done); 10 = devastating (catastrophic harm is done)
Likelihood: 1 = highly unlikely (practically impossible); 10 = highly likely (occurring frequently)
Detection: 1 = obviously detectable for easy/timely action; 10 = undetectable before action is too late
Score: Above 100 = intolerable; below 100 = moderate; below 40 = tolerable; below 20 = negligible

	Original condition (assuming no controls)					Countermeasures and resulting condition					
Ref	Risk	Effect	Severity	Likelihood	Detection	Score	Controls	Severity	Likelihood	Detection	Score	Actions	Who
R_01	Supplier failure in making timely delivery.	Disruption to service provision and reputation with customers. Contract penalties.	3	7	8	168	Supplier evaluation and management process established and maintained.	3	3	4	36	Audit effectiveness of process.	GM
R_02	ICT remote server or network failure.	Disruption to service provision and reputation. Lost custom/revenue. Contract penalties.	6	5	7	210	Support and DR process contracted to specialist. Server hardware is duplicated in separate data centres. Network data line duality. Web-based application can be operated from anywhere. 12 months guaranteed Disaster Scenario Contract.	4	1	3	12	Generally high confidence in provider but response and DR needs testing for objective proof.	ITM
R_03	Adverse weather (mainly snow ...)	Time-limited disruption to receiving supplies and ...king deliveries.	7	2	3	42	Operation located on trunk road, for better assured access. Process for ...	3	2	3	18		

Urgency of actions should reflect the risk score. Consider it irresponsible to operate systems under intolerable risk

FMEA-style risk analysis chart

The FMEA method is to, firstly, clarify (mentally or document) the function of each system component. Then investigate the potential failure modes or possible deviations from the intended performance, within each these components over the full life of the system. Ask: *"What could potentially go wrong"?*

Investigate and record the important effects on the system for each failure mode. Then further investigate to determine their root causes, by asking: *"Why did the failure happen"?* Evaluate each root cause potential in terms of severity, likelihood and ease of detection. The 3 characteristics are scored on a scale from 1 to 10, and multiplied to produce a Risk Priority Number (RPN), which signifies the magnitude of risk.

- Severity rates the adversity of the failure effect (if it occurs), where 1 = failure effect is negligible (no harm done) and 10 = devastating (severe harm is done).

- Occurrence relates to the likelihood that the root cause of the failure mode will occur, where 1 = highly unlikely (almost impossible) and 10 = highly likely (frequent).

- Detection relates to the difficulty in catching and fixing the failure before it reaches the customer, where 1 = not difficult at all and 10 = undetectable beforehand.

Determine and record the countermeasures and then re-assess the resulting RPN for the failure now being realised. An RPN of 20 or less is generally acceptable and 40 or less may be tolerated. For example, if severity is high, say a full 10, then we would want to assure that sufficient controls are put in place to make occurrence and detection scores their lowest. If, on the other hand, severity is negligibly low, then we can practically tolerate investing less in the associated controls, allowing a higher score for occurrence and detection. Residual risks are those remaining after the control measures have been implemented.

BUSINESS CONTINUITY

It should always be assumed that there are disruptions and disruptive trends going on within and around any organisation all of the time. Example origins in disruption:

- Financial and currency markets.
- Human error.
- Natural disasters.
- Physical security (theft or vandalism).
- Sudden changes in customer taste.
- Legal requirements and compliance regimes.
- Competitor innovations.
- Supply-chain and sales channel relationships.
- Intellectual property rights.
- Cyber-attacks.
- IT disaster and information loss.
- Loss of key personnel.

Business Continuity is defined as the *"capability of the organisation to continue delivery of products and services at acceptable predefined levels following a disruptive incident"* (source: ISO 22301). It is about planning and preparing an assurance that critical functions, within all layers of the organisation, under an acute serious incident or disaster, will remain capable of either continue to operate uninterruptedly or will recover in the shortest practical time. The approach is to:

- Proactively identify the risks and establish countermeasures.
- Building resilience to uncontrollable risks.
- Plan an emergency response capability to crisis management.

The aim of resilience is to design processes in ways that they can best possible maintain their desired output under normal variability in the operating environment – i.e. making the system robust to disruptions, without seeking to control the disruptions themselves. This could, for example, involve cross-skilling people or having a back-up resource on standby, within all layers of the organisation. Resilience is further about being able to seamlessly adapt to and survive evolving changes in the operating environment, which has a lot to do with people attitudes and leadership.

EMERGENCY RESPONSE PLAN

Foreseeable controllable situations should already have been addressed in the organisation's standard operating processes and risk controls. The Emergency Response Plan is concerned with the unforeseeable situations, which may require a large degree of urgently improvised actions and therefore has potential for mistaken decisions being made.

The Emergency Response Plan should as far as practically possible provide a documented road map of predetermined optional actions. This will reduce the number and magnitude of decisions that must be made during an urgent recovery operation. The plan should predefine the authority for making improvised decisions. It could also predefine the resources and generic template solutions that can be mobilised for recovery activities within the different functional areas of the organisation. All the parties and resources should be briefed about their responsibility and authority, in case of an emergency. The plan should be periodically tested, by playing an unrehearsed emergency scenario, to verify that the organisation is best possible ready and capable of responding to any unforeseeable disruptions.

MANAGING PEOPLE-BASED SYSTEMS

Organisations tend to drift across, or flip between, the cycles of its people declining or improving in performance. Even when things are going well, something unplanned can happen that puts pressure onto the system and a sudden switch to the declining cycle can occur. Likewise, when things are going bad, a small success event can help spark a break from the decline. The positive break tends to be initially weak and must be fuelled to take hold. This is a gradual slow process. It is important to avoid any drifts into the declining cycle in the first place.

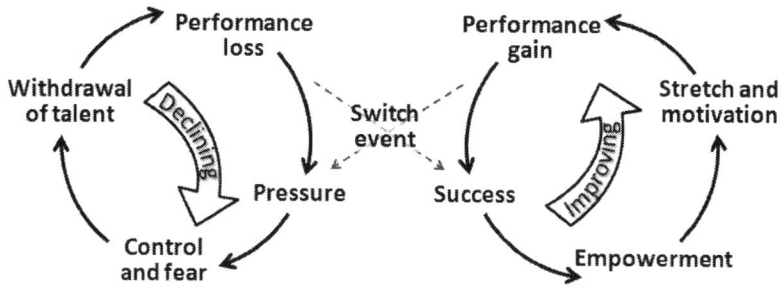

People's declining and improving performance cycles.

Generally, as long as the feeling of success is greater than that of pressure, the organisation will be moving in the right direction. Success is measured by outcomes – e.g. customer satisfaction and company result. Pressure is often linked to the forever increasing productivity demands exerted by the organisational context. But it can also arise unexpectedly – for example from a competitor establishing an unmatchable success, or from a sudden unplanned loss of a key employee or supplier. Assertive control creeps in when leaders lose their composure under the pressure, and through lack of confidence resorts to micro-managing the situation. This results in people withdrawing their discretionary talent for self-managing, and replacing it with disinterest, risk aversion and political behaviours. The declining cycle represents a pitfall that can be hard to get out of.

Pressure is not all a bad thing, because of its positive effect in enhancing the sense of success. Hard work generally feels more rewarding than light work does – up to a point. It remains important that pressure does not exceed the feeling of success.

People naturally want to do well and simply need to be allowed to do so. Under certain circumstances, at times, however, regulatory and standard requirements may demand a necessary degree of controlling governance. Optimising human resources is largely about finding a way of combining freedom and control – as well as equipping people with skills and knowledge. One way to address mandatory controls is to explain to people what the standards require, and why they therefore become important, and then most possible delegate the controlling functions to the people self.

CORPORATE VALUES STATEMENT

Values are *"inherently worthwhile and important positive qualities to a holder"*. They are rooted in personal needs, desires and ethics. Values provide meaning in the choices and decisions that we make, and in how we subsequently feel about having made them.

Clarity around the corporate values alone yields little. Without any kind of deeper personal purpose or meaning, people simply won't pay attention to a corporate value statement. Employee value-based action can never be taken for granted. Lack of a believable connection between the corporate and individual values creates a mental distance, with individuals not investing their discretionary talent and energy in the management system. In bad scenarios, employees can feel they don't fully 'belong' in the organisation. What matters most to an individual can end up competing with what is most important to the management system and, worse, to its customers. A conflict in values can thereby become value-destroying.

Importantly, for optimally leveraging the commitments of people, and to thereby optimally managing the integrated system, the organisation's values should be expressed in a language that is easy 'alignable' to people's personal values. People must also be clear about their own personal values, and how these connect and contribute to those of the organisation, before they can be able to commit to making principle-based decisions – i.e. to move beyond self-interest; to elevate the status of their work; to serve a greater good of the organisation and its customers.

Collective values, such as those held by the organisation and its customer society, are largely impersonal needs, which have to be promoted in ways that they do not conflict with personal values. Fortunately, most deeply held personal values tend to be rather stable and stay clustered around a few core themes that are compatible with those of society in general.

SELF-MANAGING UNITS

Information flow and decision-making are best integrated into the operational teams, as opposed to the teams continually relying and waiting on management intervention. This increases speed and responsiveness. In the real world, some degree of management intervention is unavoidable, but it can be reduced or translated into being more of a supporting/facilitating function. Leaders should display confidence and trust in letting people take on difficult tasks and resist stepping in to take over control (in fear of failure). This allows the individual team members to build self-confidence and it will grow the ownership of outcomes and problems. The more that teams manage themselves, at the operational level, the more capacity the senior management team has to focus on the important corporate strategic activities level. Senior management involvement in change decisions can be substituted for by governance and diligence testing devices, such as periodic reporting and internal auditing.

True improvement is achieved by people having the freedom to do right – as opposed to people being merely controlled, to guard against doing wrong. Self-managing teams are thereby better at improving and can be more resilient to exceptions/disruptions. Resilience is achieved by teams becoming self-improving, self-changing and self-healing.

TEAM BOARD

The team board is an example self-management tool, providing a focal point for the operational team. The team board could, for example, contain:

- KPIs and trends that the team is addressing.
- Resources cover information/reminders.
- Process checks (self-auditing) recording.
- Space for immediate recording of issues, errors and faults.
- Actions list and status.

The team board places relevant information and decision-points where the improvements are best made. It provides clarity and relevance to team targets and expectations. The team itself controls this information, with individual authority to add or annotate information to the board. The board could be used as the gathering point for daily or weekly team meetings. The team leader refreshes the information sheets monthly. Removed sheets can be kept on file, as a record and evidence of past activities.

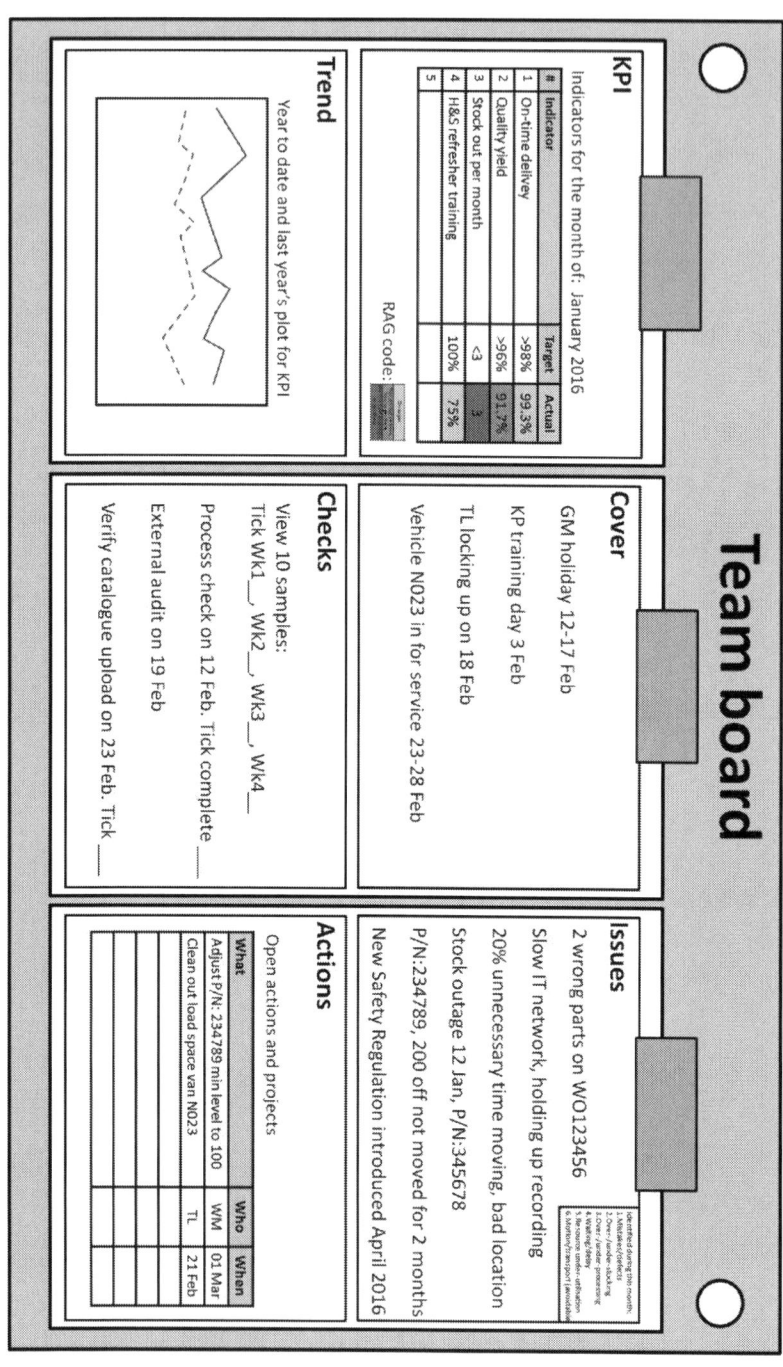

Example team board consisting of 3 x A4 information sheets.

Cascading down 3 to 5 KPIs onto the team board helps drive the organisation's objectives for the integrated management system. The RAG (Red, Amber, Green) colour code ratings can be used for visualising the team's approach to managing the KPIs.

Code	Meaning	Consequence
Green	On-target or achieved	Reason for celebration; but it also means an opportunity for being more ambitious and stretching the target.
Amber	Not there yet, but know how to	Good status that drives improvement. It is a recognised opportunity for improving the processes or outcomes.
Red	Do not yet know how to achieve	Threat of failure, which requires new (blameless) thinking, or a justified call for review of the unrealistic strategic objective behind the target.

Senior managers can relate to the operation through the team boards. For example, the manager can create urgency by showing interest in and querying the team board during walk-about in the workplace. If made cleverly, the team's line manager can physically carry and present the team board at the organisation's regular management reviews, on behalf of the team. If something does not appear to progress as expected, the team or the team manager should be asked *"can you make it green in one month, or do you need someone to step in to support"*. If necessary, the senior management can send in an 'expert' resource to help identify the root causes and the needed actions for the team.

GLOSSARY AND DEFINITIONS

ISO	International Standards Organisation
ISO 9001	International standard on requirements for quality management systems
QMS	Quality Management System
Customer	Anyone who receives products or services (outputs). Can be either people or organisations and can be either external or internal to the supplying organisation. Examples of customers include clients, consumers, users, guests, patients, purchasers, and beneficiaries.
VOC	Voice Of Customer
Product	A tangible or intangible output that is the result of a process.
Service	A form of product that is not a tangible object.
	When realised at the customer interface, service conformity with requirements cannot always be confirmed before its delivery, as is normally always possible for a tangible product.
Organisation	People and facilities arranged to achieve objectives by using its functions, responsibilities, authorities and relationships. It can be a company, corporation, enterprise, partnership, sole trader, charity, association or institution and can be either privately or publicly owned.

Policy	Overall intentions and direction of an organisation as formally expressed by top management.
Objective	Something sought, or aimed for.
Management	Coordinated activities to direct and control an organisation.
System	Set of interrelated or interacting elements that do something together.
Management system	A system that formulates policies and objectives and establishes the processes that are needed to ensure that policies are followed and objectives are achieved.
Document	Information and its supporting medium – e.g. electronic, printed or hand written text, drawing, flow chart or pictures.
Record	Document stating results achieved or providing evidence of activities performed.
Quality	Degree to which a set of inherent characteristics fulfils requirements, where characteristic means distinguishing feature that is inherent or assigned, qualitative or quantitative, and where requirement means need or expectation that is stated, generally implied or obligatory.
Satisfaction	Perception of the degree to which the requirements have been fulfilled. Note: Absence of complaints does not necessarily imply satisfaction.

ABOUT THE AUTHOR

Frede Jensen has 20 years of senior management experiences, including with responsibilities for innovation, process design and quality in manufacturing and the service sector, within private, public, small and global businesses. He has an MSc in Quality Engineering Management, is IQA Lead Auditor trained and a Six Sigma Black Belt. In the last 8 years, he has worked with a mix of commercial and academic organisations, as an independent consultant in design and quality management.

Other book by Frede Jensen:

Quality Function Deployment:
  The evolved 4-phase model
Published 2017
English
76 pages
ISBN 978-1-326-90591-0

This book presents the 4-phase Quality Function Deployment (QFD) model. The model assures quality-by-design and can reduce project time costs. It is essential knowledge for design and system developers. The approach is applicable to the development of anything, including products, parts, materials, services, events, software and websites. The 4-phase model meets the ISO 16355-1:2015 guidance standard. The House of Quality is explained, as a specification and planning tool for transferring the priorities in customer and stakeholder requirements into a final producible product.

Appendix

a) Summary Audit Checklist (pages 82-83) for performing a high-level health check on an organisation's system.

b) Process Check form for a team self-sampling its conformity.

c) Example process definitions for:
   i. Strategy deployment.
   ii. Risk and continuity.
   iii. Management review.
   iv. Internal auditing.
   v. Feedback.
   vi. Proactive and reactive corrections.
   vii. Competencies management.
   viii. Supplier management.
   ix. Occupational health and safety.
   x. Production.
   xi. Document control.
   xii. Records control.
   xiii. Programme management.

The process definitions here are kept to a minimum in details, to facilitate their fit onto a single book page. Each process should incorporate requirements for all the standards that are being integrated. The processes may well be documented differently in differing organisations.

Find more detailed process definition examples and templates at: www.deopmanagement.com/process_manual.html

Organisation appreciation and observations record sheet.

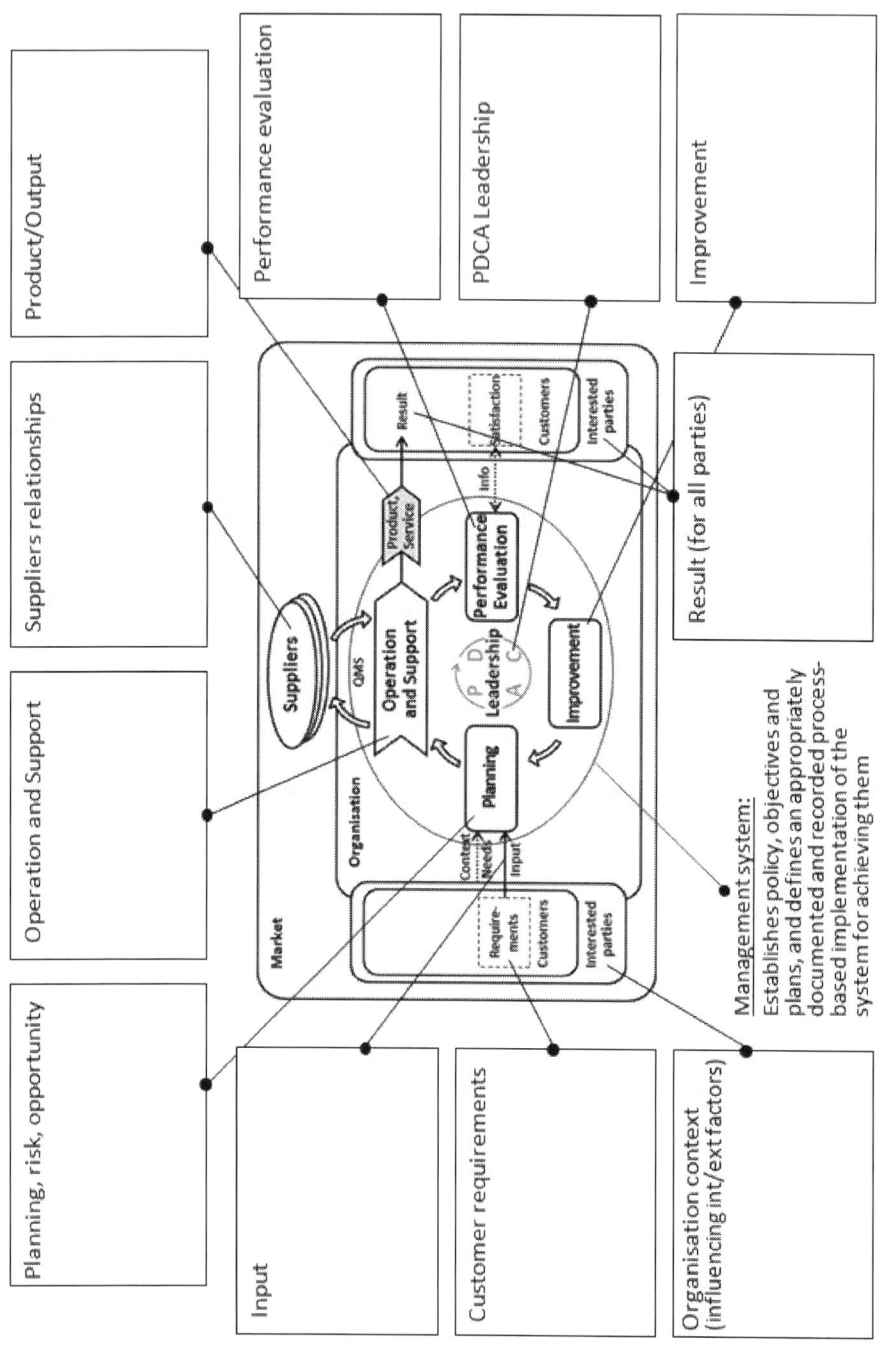

Checklist for summary audit against ISO general system model.

Score	Description
0	Non-existent
1	Initial or ad-hoc
2	Repeatable, intuitive
3	Defined
4	Managed, measured
5	Optimised, excellent

Management System Requirement	Score	Observation
Customers, stakeholders, relevant standards and regulatory requirements are all understood.		
Organisation's objectives are defined to meet requirements, planned and communicated to all.		
Management system, policies and important processes are defined, documented and accessible to all.		
Regular management reviews are recorded/evidenced and actions satisfy the objectives/plan.		
Resources are managed and sufficiently developed/competent in supporting objectives/plan.		
Operational and support processes satisfy the input requirements and specification.		
Suppliers are managed in effective relationships.		
Systems are measured, audited, evaluated, improved. Evidence of leadership driving the PDCA cycle.		
There is evidence of customer satisfaction, together with absence of dissatisfaction.		
Adopted standards and regulatory requirements are met.		

Self-managing team's process check record.

Process Check

Department:	Date:
Team:	Assessor:

This is a standard form, using generic terms. The word 'work item' below refers to any piece of work, whether, for example, a physical assembly, a written document or a computer entry. It can be a complete finished item or a sub-part or sub-assembly for a bigger item. Cross out incorrect options.

Item 1

Description:	Complete item / Sub-part of bigger item		
Traceable reference to the sample reviewed			
How much of the team's work time/emphasis is spent on this kind of work item			%
All people working on the item have received appropriate and sufficient training		Yes	No
Sample viewed is worked correctly, considering the process and any work instruction		Yes	No
Quality of completion of sample viewed is acceptable, considering customer viewpoint		Yes	No
Speed of completion is acceptable, considering customer and company viewpoint		Yes	No
Work documents are adequate to assure a trained person can complete correctly		Yes	No
Any work document or instruction is followed correctly		Yes	No

Item 2

Description:	Complete item / Sub-part of bigger item		
Traceable reference to the sample reviewed			
How much of the team's work time/emphasis is spent on this kind of work item			%
All people working on the item have received appropriate and sufficient training		Yes	No
Sample viewed is worked correctly, considering the process and any work instruction		Yes	No
Quality of completion of sample viewed is acceptable, considering customer viewpoint		Yes	No
Speed of completion is acceptable, considering customer and company viewpoint		Yes	No
Work documents are adequate to assure a trained person can complete correctly		Yes	No
Any work document or instruction is followed correctly		Yes	No

Item 3

Description:	Complete item / Sub-part of bigger item		
Traceable reference to the sample reviewed			
How much of the team's work time/emphasis is spent on this kind of work item			%
All people working on the item have received appropriate and sufficient training		Yes	No
Sample viewed is worked correctly, considering the process and any work instruction		Yes	No
Quality of completion of sample viewed is acceptable, considering customer viewpoint		Yes	No
Speed of completion is acceptable, considering customer and company viewpoint		Yes	No
Work documents are adequate to assure a trained person can complete correctly		Yes	No
Any work document or instruction is followed correctly		Yes	No

Previous Process Checks

To ensure all types of work items are reviewed over a reasonable cycle, all non-trivial items should be reviewed at least once every 12 months. Please confirm the percentage of non-trivial work item types reviewed in the last 12 months.			%
Actions identified in previous audits are resolved or progressed according to plan		Yes	No

Please attach separate sheet or examples, as necessary, for providing further details

Conclusion

Actions:	Who and when:
Signed:	Date:

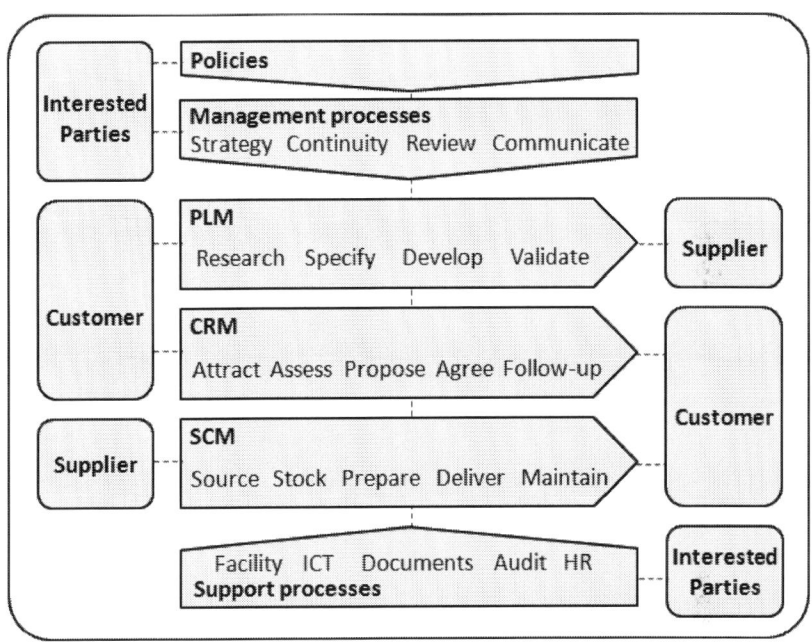

Example map of core processes

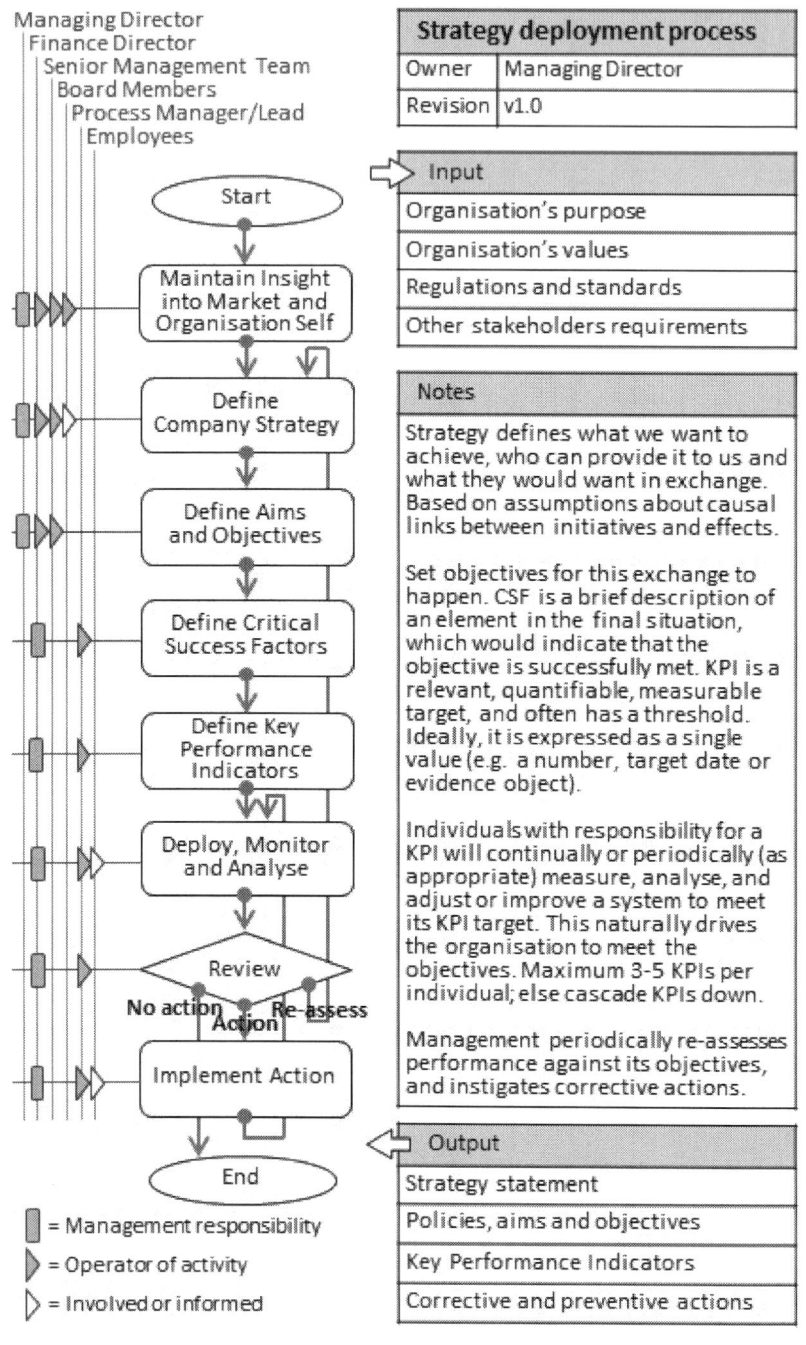

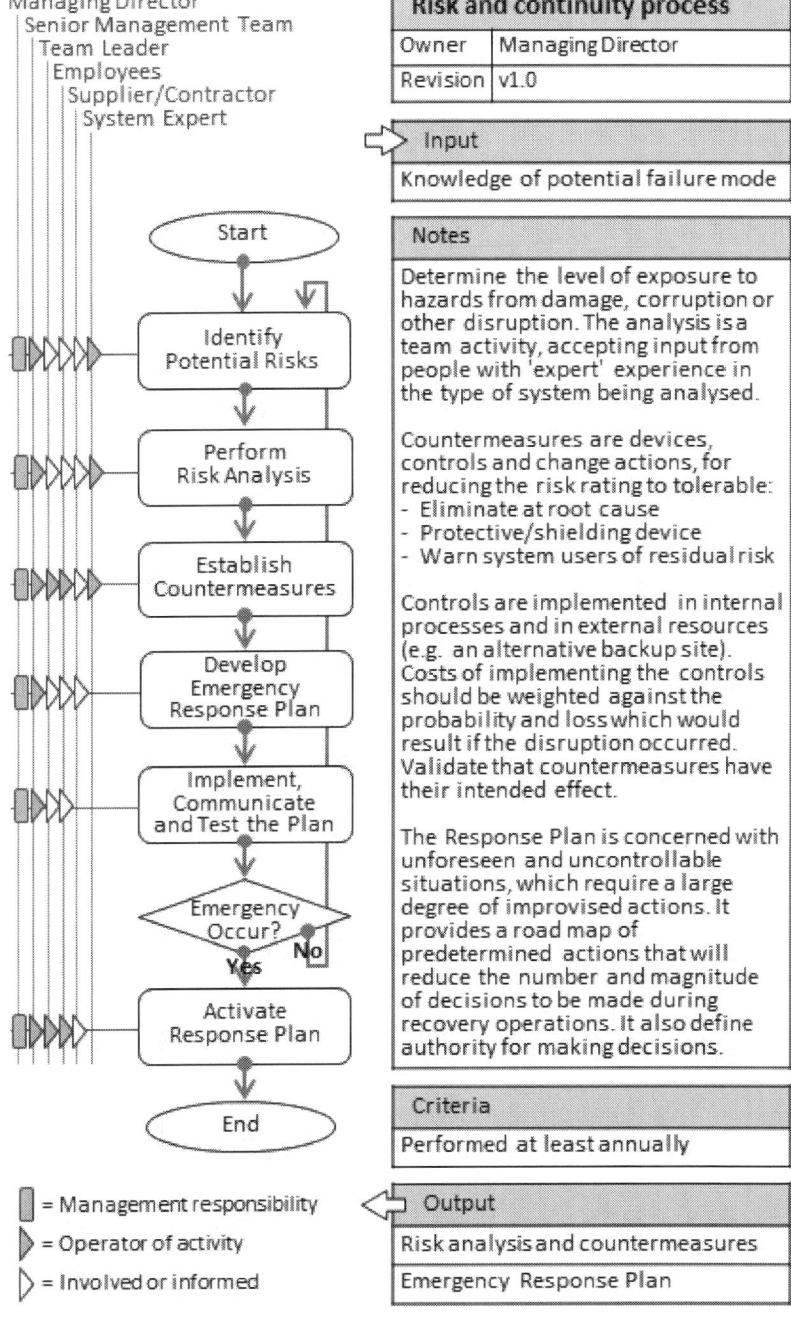

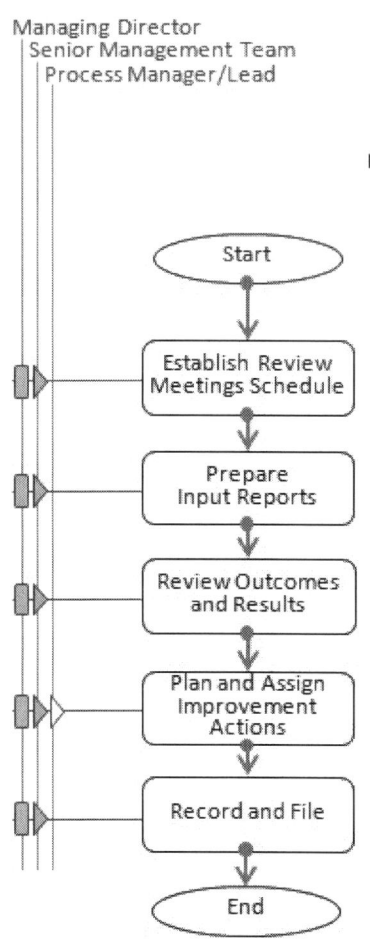

Managing Director
 Senior Management Team
  Process Manager/Lead

Management Review process	
Owner	Managing Director
Revision	v1.0

Input

Status of measures/KPIs
Status of previous review actions
Corrective and preventive actions
Market feedback and trends
Products performance/conformity
Processes performance/audits
People competencies and issues
Environmental and safety risk issues
Suppliers performances and issues
ICT and facilities

Notes

Reviews are carried out as part of the regularly planned management team meeting. Purpose is to ensure the implementation of policy and objectives, and to improve effectiveness and efficiency of the integrated management system.

Each area manager prepares input report in advance of the review.

The discussions and outcomes of the review are recorded. The rationale for not receiving a particular performance report or for not reviewing a particular input items is noted in the minutes of the meeting.

Criteria

Review held at least monthly
All areas covered over 12 months
Record kept for minimum 3 years

Output

Recorded improvement actions relating to issues in the input reports

▌ = Management responsibility
▷ = Operator of activity
▷ = Involved or informed

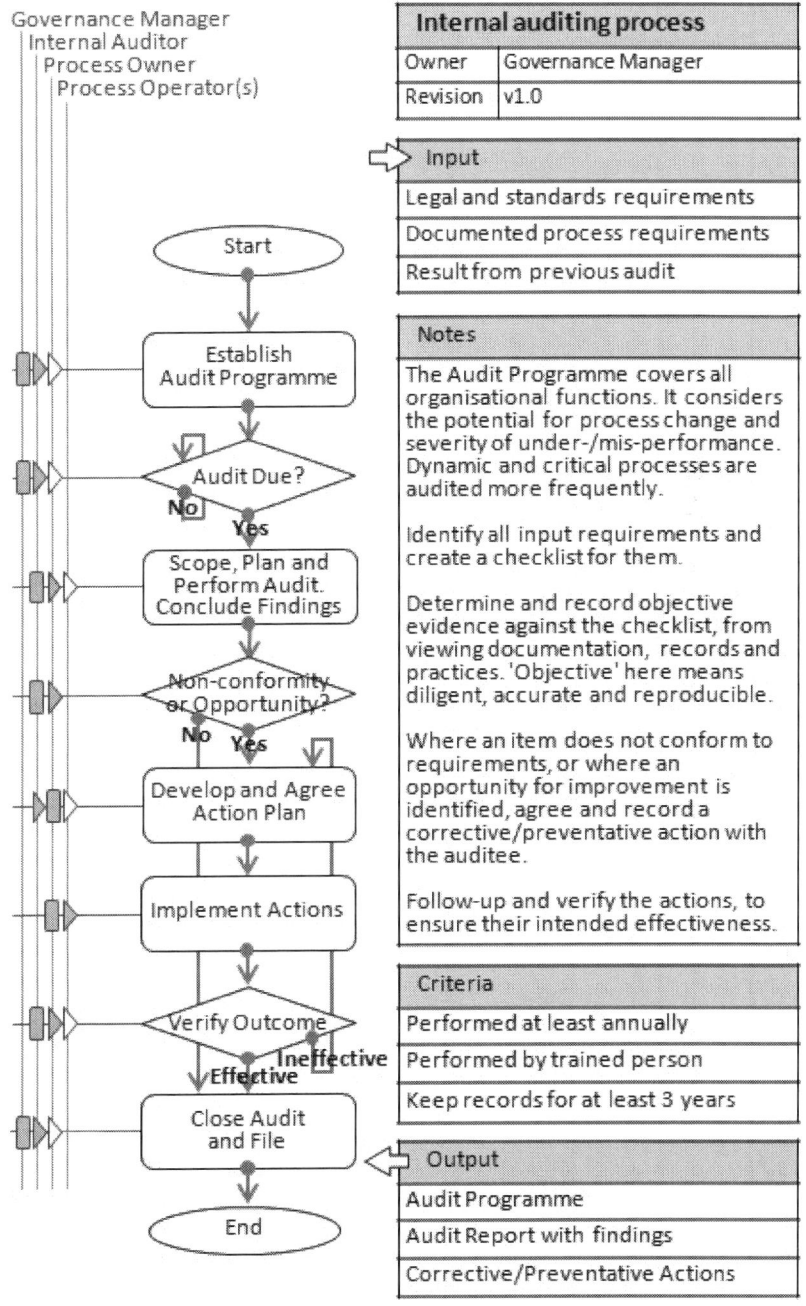

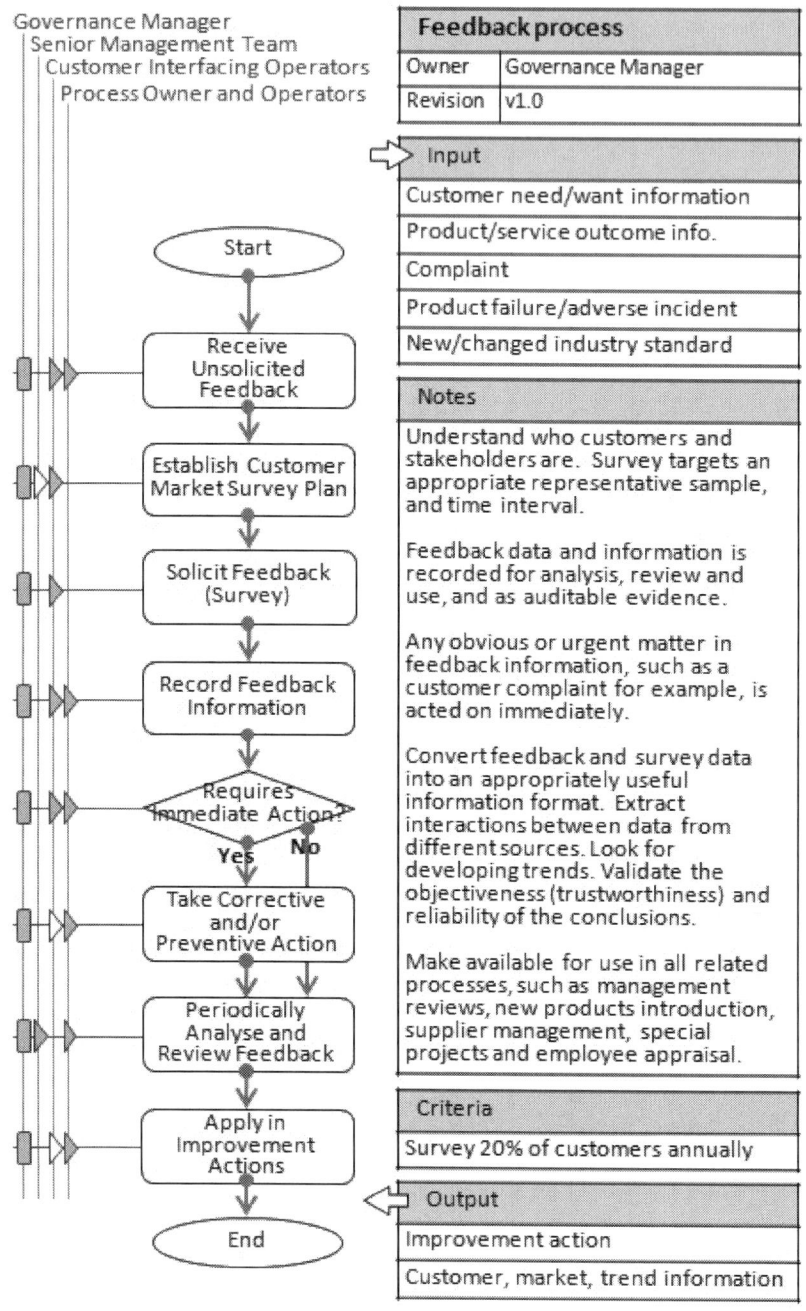

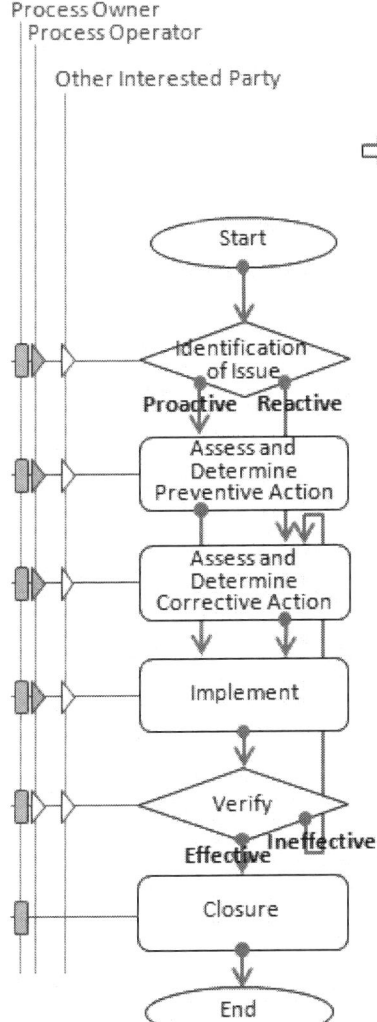

Corrective actions process	
Owner	Operations Manager
Revision	v1.0

Input
Arising problem or issue
Planned measurement data

Notes
Process owners and operators are responsible for proactively studying or soliciting suggestions to pre-empt a process fault or other dissatisfier, before it has materialised. This is the starting point for preventive action.
Process owners and operators are responsible for reactively addressing and preventing recurrence of any recognized shortfall in meeting requirements. This is the starting point for corrective action.
Gather evidence and analyse the root causes to the actual or potential failure. Develop countermeasure until the failure risk is eliminated or at an acceptable/tolerable low level.
Assign responsibility and time frame for implementing the action.
Verify that the action is effectively implemented as intended and that is has had the assumed full effect. If not, determine further actions.
Record and action and the approval of the outcome, for evidential and learning purpose.

Output
Improvement action
Approval of closure and verification

■ = Management responsibility
▷ = Operator of activity
▷ = Involved or informed

91

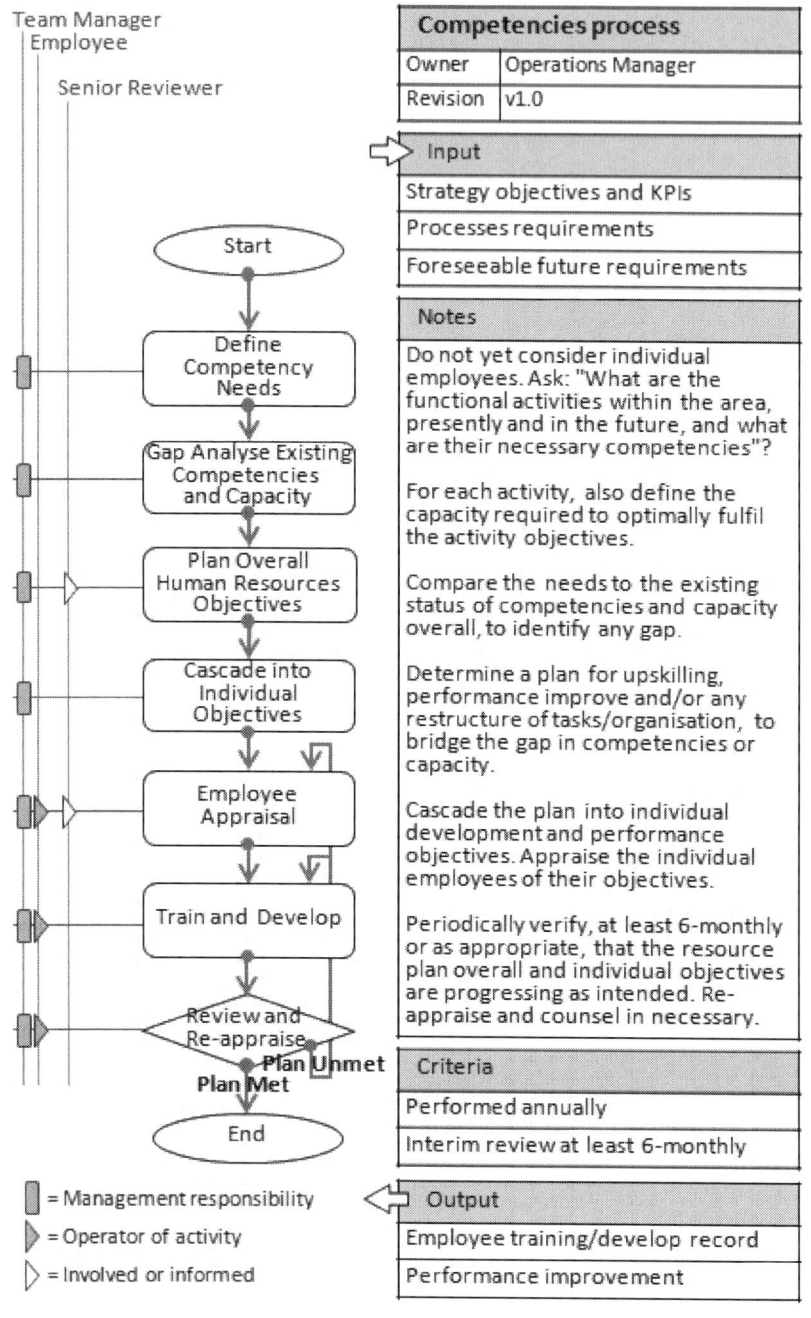

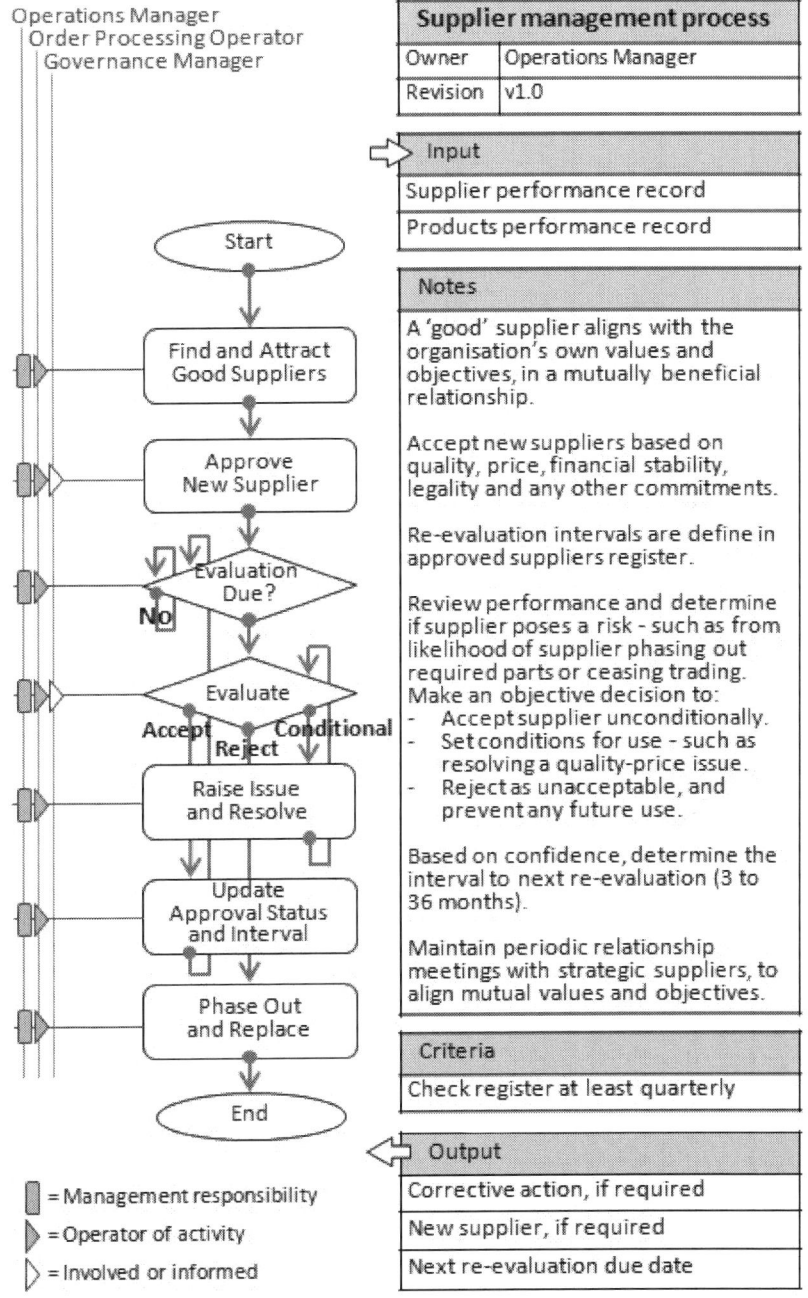

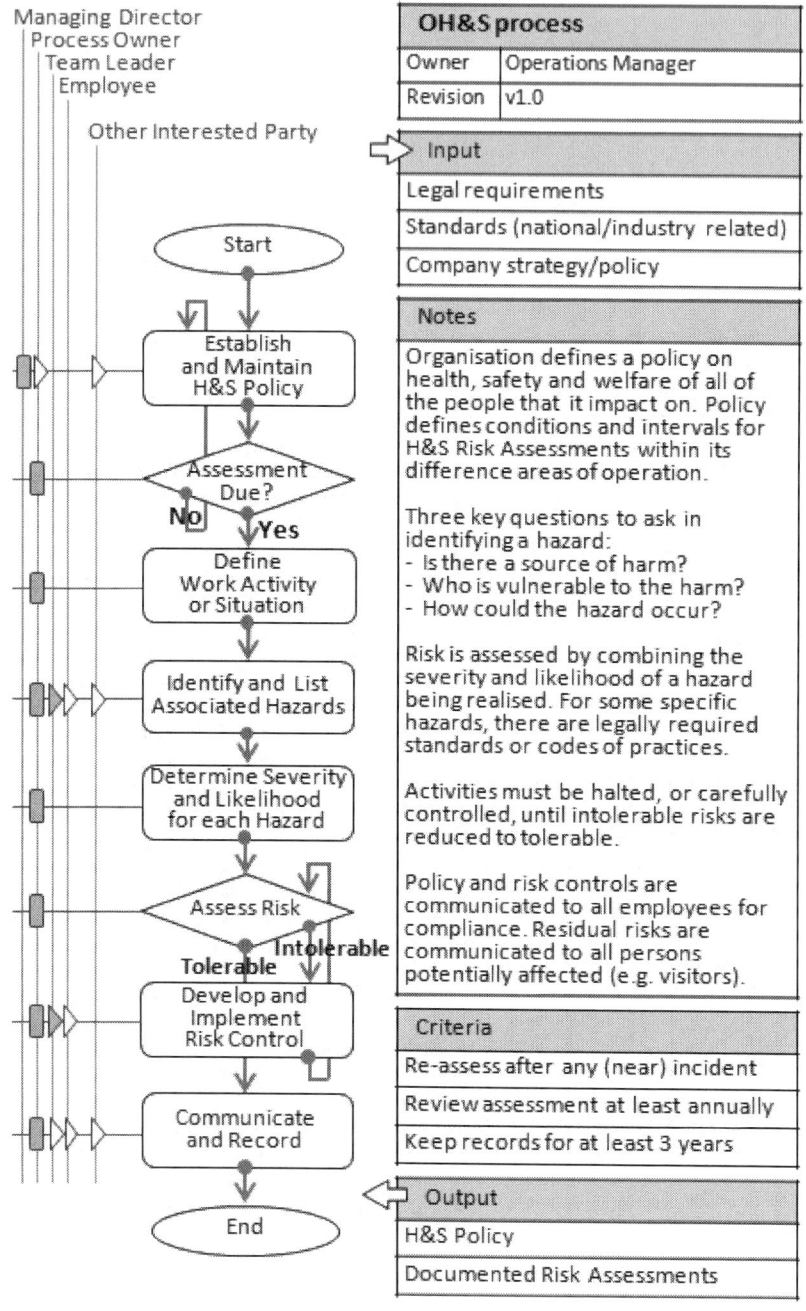

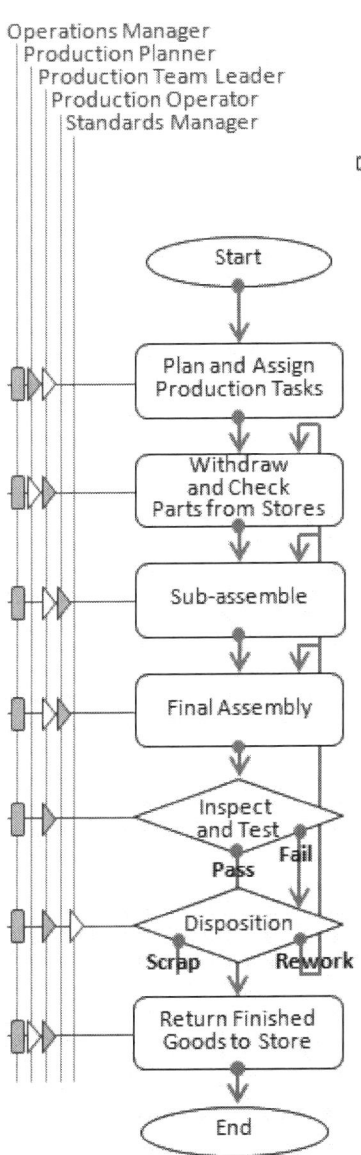

Operations Manager
  Production Planner
    Production Team Leader
      Production Operator
        Standards Manager

■ = Management responsibility
▷ = Operator of activity
▷ = Involved or informed

Production process	
Owner	Operations Manager
Revision	v1.0

Input
Production plan

Notes
Team Leader signs and issues a process card showing:
- Date of issue
- Who the batch is assigned to
- Work Order (WO) number
- Items and quantities

Assemble according to relevant Work Instructions.

Any sub-standard parts discovered (in low numbers) are scrapped set aside. The Team Leader will collect, count and return all scrapped parts to stores for replacement.

Inspection and testing equipment calibration status is verified. Test carried out to the relevant Product Test Specification. Reject Ticket is attached to any part failing to meet the requirements of the PTS.

The final release [Pass] must be authorised by a competent person with designated responsibility.

Finished, tested parts are passed to stored with the relevant traceability.

Criteria
100% to Work Instruction
>98% inspection yield
>85% resource time efficiency

Output
Products
Parts/batch traceability record
Inspection and testing record

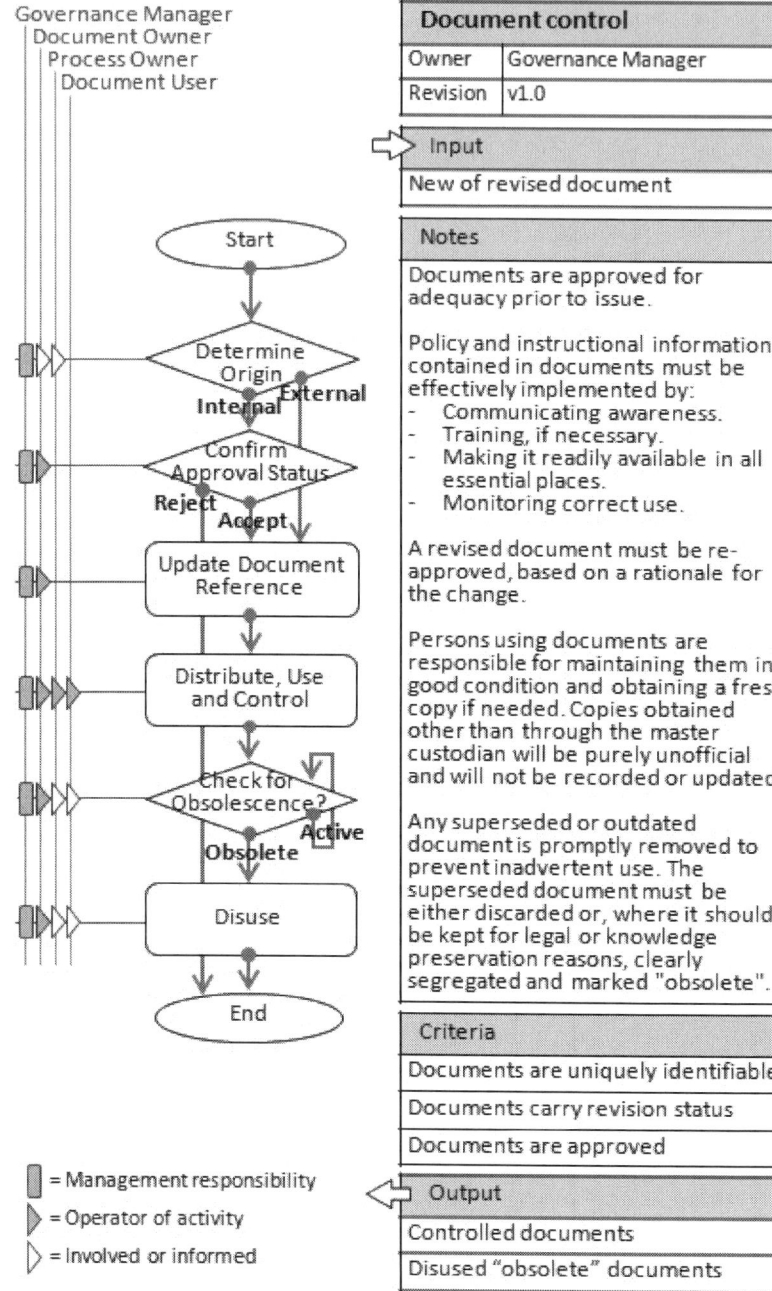

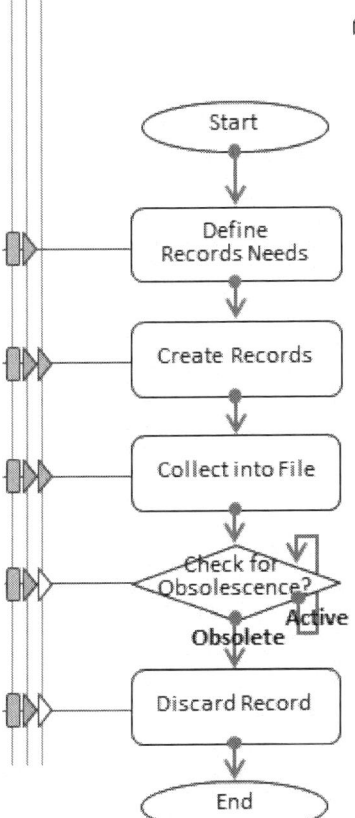

Records control	
Owner	Governance Manager
Revision	v1.0

Input

Information to be preserved

Notes

Records must be established and maintained to effectively:

a) Respond completely and promptly to customers.
b) Measure and analyse past results in all functional areas.
c) Verify approval/authority.
d) Trace individual transactions histories and details/quantities through each link (forward and backward) in the process-chain.
e) Protect against any contract or legal liability issue, by providing proof of past activities/results.

Information received in non-documented form, but which may later be relied on, must be recorded (e.g. write and date a file note).

Process managers are responsible for protecting records, including re-establishing any missing items.

Criteria

Records are identifiable, retrievable
Records are legible
Personal/confidential data is secure
Operational records kept for 5 years
Incorporation records indefinitely

Output

Records kept in readily accessible file
Records kept in archive
Obsolete records destroyed/discard.

▪ = Management responsibility
▷ = Operator of activity
▷ = Involved or informed

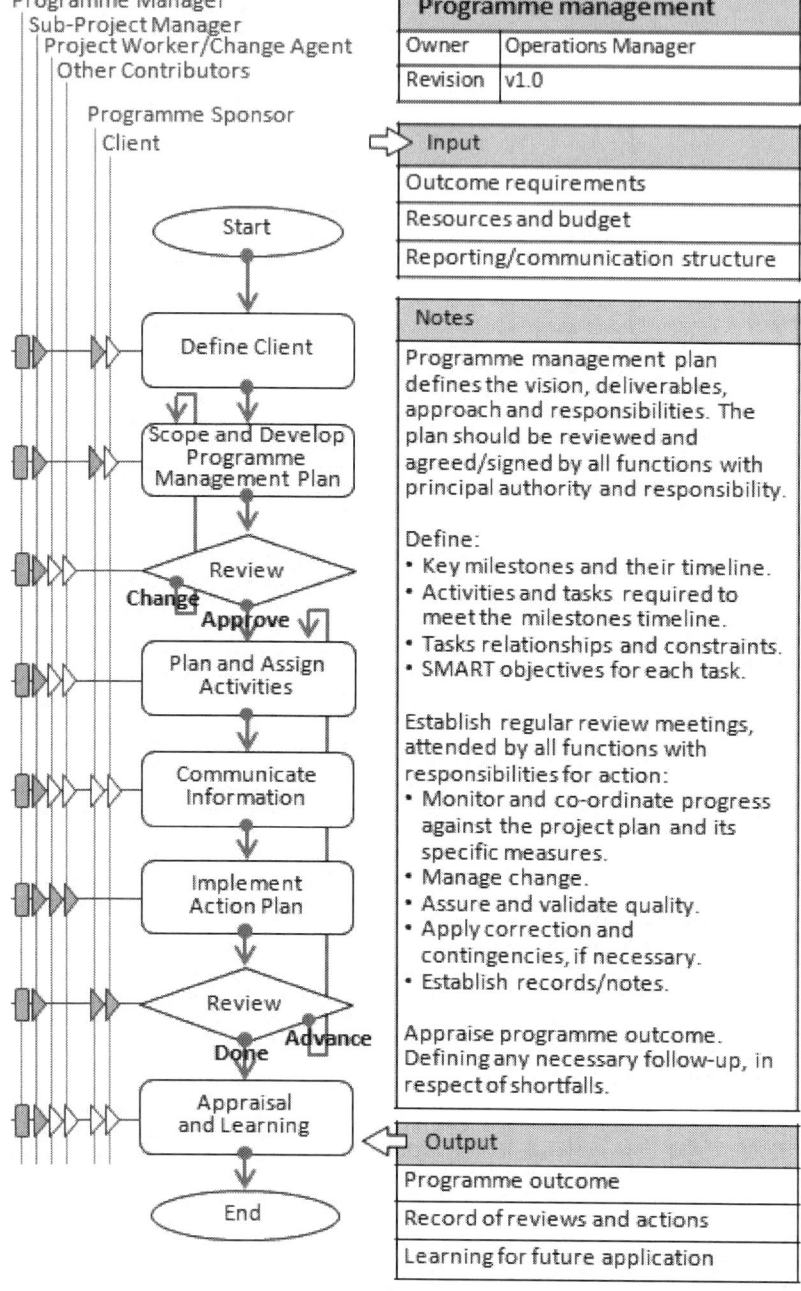

Index

Analysis 40
Auditing 33
Business continuity 70
Corporate value statement 73
Corrective action 41
Customers 44
    Dissatisfaction 48
    Needs 44
    Satisfaction 45
Documentation 31
Evidence-based decision making 38
Facilities 30
Failure Mode and Effects Analysis 67
Improvement 36
Integrated management system 4
    Checklist 82
    Documenting 57
Integrated organisation 4
Integrated process manual 57
Interested parties 44
ISO standards 50
    ISO 9001 52
    ISO 14001 54
    ISO 50001/EN 16001 55
    OHSAS 18001 56
KPIs 18, 24, 75
Leadership 22
Management review 35
Management system model 13, 82
Measurement 32
Operations 28
Opportunity 65
Organisational context 16
People 30, 72
Performance evaluation 32
Plan-Do-Check-Act 13
Planning 24
Policy deployment 24
Preventive action 41
Process approach 19
Process design 61
Process documentation 31, 57
Processes examples 85
    Competencies management 92
    Document control 95
    Feedback 90
    Internal auditing 89
    Management review 88
    Occupational Health & Safety 94
    Proactive and reactive corrections 91
    Production process 95
    Programme management 98
    Records control 97
    Risk and continuity 87
    Supplier management 93
    Strategy deployment 86
Risk and opportunity 65
Risk management 66
Self-checks (conformity auditing) 34, 84
Self-managing units 74
Standards, why adopt 10
Suppliers 42
Support processes 30
Targets, setting 28
Team board 75

Printed in Great Britain
by Amazon